AS YOU WALK ALONG THE WAY

The word "unique" best describes *As You Walk Along the Way*. It provides valuable insights, encouragements and suggestions into helping parents train children in spiritual disciplines. But its content does not promote forcing children into legalistic practices; rather it offers helpful ideas that come from both Scripture and experience. A must read for parents who want to raise children who love God with all their hearts.

—Jonathan Graf,
Editor, *Pray!*

As You *Walk* Along the *Way*

How to Lead Your Child on the Path of Spiritual Discipline

Carla R. Williams

HORIZON BOOKS
CAMP HILL, PENNSYLVANIA

HORIZON BOOKS

3825 Hartzdale Drive, Camp Hill, PA 17011
www.cpi-horizon.com
www.christianpublications.com

As You Walk Along the Way
ISBN: 0-88965-187-6

LOC Control Number: 00-135127

Dedicated to my Heavenly Father,
who set the example of the perfect Parent.

And to Tim, my friend, my husband and my master,
whose steadfast trust in the Lord kept me from giving in
to fear as we walked with our children.

*For this is the way the holy women of the past who put their
hope in God used to make themselves beautiful. They were
submissive to their own husbands, like Sarah, who obeyed
Abraham and called him her master. You are her daughters
if you do what is right and do not give way to fear.* (1 Peter
3:5-6)

Contents

FOREWORD

Many parenting books focus on how to get our children to do the good things that good children are supposed to do. That's because our parenting focuses so much on outward behavior. We tell our kids to say "thank you" to Grandma (which is OK), but too often we don't consider how to help our child cultivate a thankful heart. Then a child automatically says "thank you" and might not even mean it.

The consequence of parents focusing on external behavior while ignoring the inner person is enormous. Lack of attention to the soul produces a child whose behavior reflects godly values, but whose heart is numb to God.

But, you object, the trick with training a child's heart is that it's difficult to measure. This is true, but it doesn't make the spiritual formation of the soul less important. What, exactly, then is spiritual formation? It is "using certain practices to cultivate an inner life that is strongly connected to God. This inward life results in the transformation of our outward behavior. Through this process, we become disciples of Jesus Christ imitating both His inward heart attitudes and His outward behavior."

But how does spiritual formation occur? Growth in Christlikeness occurs as we use certain accepted practices described in the Bible and practiced by Jesus. Just as a future concert pianist uses techniques and practices to train herself for the intended goal, a believer can benefit greatly from the practice of "spiritual disciplines." These disciplines, so overlooked today, create back-and-forth contact with God— allowing God to transform our character and personality to resemble His own. They're not very difficult—really. They're simply about learning to connect with God.

Carla Williams (along with her husband Tim) chose to incorporate these spiritual disciplines into the way she has raised her children. In this book, she shares those ideas with us in practical ways that she tried out herself.

You may think your own use of spiritual disciplines is so paltry that you could never motivate, much less teach, your children to use them. But consider that the opposite may be true. Teaching our children spiritual disciplines—making them so simple and down-to-earth that even a child can figure them out and like doing them—may be just the key in learning to use them yourself.

Many years ago I felt the need to have a richer discipline of personal worship in my life. My children were preschoolers and so I experimented with helping them learn to do this. One evening as my five-year-old son and I sat on the front porch steps, I pointed out the glowing sunset to him and he yelped, "Yay, God!" His spontaneous ability to worship God drew me in. I joined him, "Yes, yay, God!" and began clapping. His exuberance set an example for me.

Yet my attempts could have been so much better with help such as Carla gives in this book. While reading her manuscript, I caught myself thinking, I need to start over and try all this! So maybe I'll try them with my grandchildren someday. My prayer is that you'll enjoy this time with Carla.

Jan Johnson
author of *When the Soul Listens*
and *Growing Compassionate Kids*

ACKNOWLEDGMENTS

♥ First I want to thank my Lord for counting me worthy enough to show me the secrets of raising children in His presence. Thanks to my husband, Tim, for lovingly keeping me on the narrow path to the cross. And to all my children, especially Joshua and Josiah, for their patience as I learned the secrets for raising godly children. A big thanks to my great-grandfather Ray, who told me, "Always love Jesus," and to his daughter, my Granny, who taught me how, so that I could pass it onto her great-grandchildren and great-great grandchildren.

♥ Special thanks to my friend Lin Johnson, who kept reminding me that "The Lord has a time for this book." Thanks to the girls in my Colorado critique group for their help and encouragement: Alice Scott Ferguson, Marianne Herring, Nancy Parker Brummett, Elisabeth Hendricks, Jeannie Harmon, Sheila Seifert, Liz Duckworth and especially Jeanne Dennis (for all her hours of editing by e-mail). And to Liza, Julie and Tammy for making sure my i's were dotted and my t's were crossed.

♥ A big hug to Gloria Myers, Athena and Tia Dean and little Ezekiel for being my Mommy and Grandma test market. A special thanks to Erin Healy, the editor who published my articles on encouraging children to have quiet times, validating this book, but cared enough to practice the ideas with her daughter Amber.

♥ Finally, to my editor David Fessenden, who looked past the roadblocks and had a heart for guiding children down the path of spiritual discipline. Thank you for working so hard at helping me keep the message of loving God with all your heart, soul, mind and strength the center of this book.

INTRODUCTION

Nine out of ten marriages resulting from an unwanted pregnancy end within the first year," announced newscaster Walter Cronkite. My heart sank. *Great! We've only been married a week and the odds are already against us!* I glanced at my husband, Tim, who smiled as if to reassure me it wouldn't happen to us. His father and mother, who had graciously provided us a home, cheerfully tried to change the subject. Yet in spite of all the reassurance, I couldn't help wondering what guarantees we had of not becoming a statistic.

Conceiving my first child out of wedlock sprang motherhood on me before I was ready. Even after accepting the forgiveness of Christ, seeking God's will about having children never crossed my mind. One child was enough for me. Only God's grace brought my husband and me to a place of surrender, especially about whether or not to have more children.

At the onset of our Christian walk, Tim and I became houseparents of a group home for mentally disabled adults. During our three years there we cared for a total of twenty-three men. When the time came to leave, we were ready for a break. Having more children was not in our plans. Yet, the Lord seemed to tug on our hearts. The Psalmist tells us:

Sons are a heritage from the LORD,
    children a reward from him.
Like arrows in the hands of a warrior
    are sons born in one's youth.

> Blessed is the man
> whose quiver is full of them.
> (Psalm 127:3-5)

Burned out from the group home experience, I especially longed for a reprieve and had no desire to fill my *quiver* with children. But in the first verse of this passage I saw that, "Unless the LORD builds the house, its builders labor in vain" (127:1).

Now why do you suppose David wrote these two passages together? Obviously the Lord would like to have some say about when and how many, *if any*, children couples should bring into the world. Tim and I decided that we did not want to leave this area of our lives up to chance or our own opinions. So we made a commitment to seek God's will about how many children we should bring into this world.

It took several days of prayer and fasting to surrender to the idea that the time had come to enlarge our family. The Lord softened our hearts and we soon conceived Joshua. Two years later we were blessed with a third son. After Josiah we knew that the time for child bearing had ended. Yet, by now my attitude had changed and I wanted a "quiver full." Little did I know that in the years to follow, the Lord would bring more than twenty-five children temporarily into our home.

Now that my children are almost grown, I can reflect on the lessons the Lord taught us through our roles as parents. As I share the ways God has brought our family into His presence, I never want to give the impression it was always easy. Parenting is a tough job. And in this day and age, raising godly children is even tougher.

As You Walk Along the Way strives to be a companion to parents who desire to encourage their children to walk with God in very intimate and personal ways. When I first started writing this book many, many years ago, my goal was to give parents ideas on how to encourage their children to love God with all their hearts, souls, minds and strengths (Deuteronomy 6:5; Luke 10:27). But as in all things, when we surrender to God's timing, He usually has lessons for us to learn before we can share with others. Tim and I had a lot more to discover about surrendering our children to Him completely. As time passed, and with it many publishers' rejection letters, it became apparent that the way God had taught us to teach our kids to love Him was through the practice of the spiritual disciplines.

As God sifted Tim's and my parenting skills and the self that we hung on to, the chaff fell away and the spiritual disciplines rose to the top. Guiding our children in the disciplines such as prayer, worship and meditation gave us a light for the path we walked with our children.

> For these commands are a lamp,
>   this teaching is a light,
> and the corrections of discipline
>   are the way to life. (Proverbs 6:23)

Walter Cronkite was right. Marriages based on an unwanted pregnancy usually end in divorce and the children are the ones who suffer. Our marriage had many obstacles to overcome. Setting priorities of God first and family second didn't work. That only left us feeling guilty and frustrated when we couldn't live up to our goals. When Tim and I quit trying to improve our marriage and the way we raised our children, we discovered that our love for each other grew the more we fell in love with the Lord. Realizing and accepting that God is indeed a jealous God who demands all our devotion freed us to allow His love to flow through us. Today I would love to tell Mr. Cronkite, "Thanks to the Lord, *that's the way it is.*"

Throughout this book I share stories from the experiences of our family and friends. I've changed some of the names for the sake of privacy. My prayer is that you will also find hope in the pages that follow and that you will learn the joy that my husband and I found in walking with our children along the path of spiritual discipline.

Chapter One

PANTY HOSE SCRIPTURES

Roamie, Roamie, where'd you get that saddle? A horse ran away with a forty dollar saddle!" Granny sang as she bounced me on her knee. I squealed as she dropped me toward the floor, knowing she would catch me every time. Our cozy hideaway consisted of a small chair placed over a furnace grate. Warm air forced from the creaking furnace in the basement and a door to an adjacent room sheltered us from the cold drafts of the old house and the rest of the world.

After several rounds of giggles and horsey rides, Granny would lead a chorus of "Jesus Loves Me" or "The B-I-B-L-E." A Bible story or her childhood memories filled the rest of our "you and me" time. Granny always said that her grandchildren never grew too big for her small lap. Yet as I learned to read independently, she encouraged me to find a quiet place of my own to read the Bible or classic books. Scripture verses written on pieces of cardboard (taken from packages of panty hose) covered Granny's kitchen walls. Volumes of spiral notebooks stored her journals and thoughts which she often shared. My grandmother certainly knew the meaning of the command:

Love the LORD your God with all your heart and with all your soul and with all your strength. These commandments

1

that I give you today are to be upon your hearts. Impress
them on your children. Talk about them when you sit at
home and when you walk along the road, when you lie down
and when you get up. Tie them as symbols on your hands and
bind them on your foreheads. Write them on the doorframes
of your houses and on your gates. (Deuteronomy 6:5-9)

Such memories flooded my mind the day my two-year-old son burst
into my personal devotional time. I had recently renewed my commitment to God to have a daily time in prayer and Bible reading. To protect the time, I kept Mark occupied by training him to have his own
"quiet time"—sending him to another room to pray or read a book. On
this particular morning he interrupted me to announce that he had spoken to Moses. I laughed and brushed it off as I sent my son back to his
room.

After returning to my own prayer closet, I pondered Mark's procla-
mation. I suddenly realized how much he needed more spiritual guidance. My husband Tim and I couldn't leave this part of our son's life up
to his Sunday school teachers or to chance.

As I thought of the expression on my son's face at seeing Moses, I
recalled Granny's "panty hose Scriptures." In the midst of that warm,
cozy room, those pieces of cardboard "impressed" the Word of God
upon my heart. Acts 17:24, 26-27 tells us,

The God who made the world and everything in it . . .
made every nation of men, that they should inhabit the whole
earth; and he determined the times set for them and the exact
places where they should live. God did this so that men
would seek him and perhaps reach out for him and find him,
though he is not far from each one of us.

God placed me in Granny's family so that I would cuddle on her lap,
sing songs, read her walls and someday cry out to Him. Likewise, the
Lord had left Mark in Tim's and my care. My son's "Moses experi-

ence" helped me realize that the time had come to take the spiritual aspects of my mothering role seriously. As parents, raising our children consists of much more than clothing, feeding and entertaining them. God has placed your children or grandchildren in your family so that they too will cry out to Him.

The spiritual disciplines that Granny taught went beyond memorizing Bible verses and stories. She demonstrated by her life the importance of simplicity and times of solitude. Teaching me to journal led to prayer, meditation and study of God's Word. The affectionate childhood games instilled faith and trust. Mark's "close encounter of the spiritual kind" stirred within me a strong desire to pass on Granny's legacy to my own children and grandchildren. *If Granny could write the Scriptures on the "door frames" of her house, so could I. But how? My panty hose came in plastic eggs!*

After I shared the morning's experience with Tim, we made a commitment to establish a habit of daily devotional time with Mark. Spiritual transformation, however, is not formed by human will and determination. How many times in my life had I strived to develop a habit of a daily quiet time? How often had I failed at trying to gain self-control in eating or breaking other unhealthy habits? I didn't want the same thing to happen with this resolution. Righteousness is a free gift of grace through Jesus Christ (Romans 5:17). Yet God has asked me to do my part by implementing the disciplines of the Spirit, such as prayer, meditation and studying His Word. I understood that God was the Keeper of my child's soul and heart, but I had a part to play, too. Like my grandmother, I wanted to pass these things on to my children in a natural way.

Meditating on the passage in Deuteronomy, I imagined Israelite parents using the stars, rocks and trees as lesson props. I began to realize I could also use the things at hand to teach biblical truths to my children. Think of what Hebrew families contended with as they exited Egypt on the way to the Promised Land. "Are we there yet? Are we there yet?" is the familiar cry from the back seat of our family car on a trip of just a few hours. For *forty years* Israelite parents had to listen to the whines and cries of their children!

"How much longer do we have to walk across this stupid desert? What do you mean, thirty-seven and a half more years? No way!"

How would a parent keep a child occupied? There would be no license plates to play "Fifty States." You would find no McDonalds along the way—only manna, day in and day out. The old familiar "potty stop" would be the first bush around the next corner. (Thank you, Lord, for placing me in the twentieth century!)

Yet think of the things an Israelite family *never* had to worry about—drugs, gang fights in school, pornography on the Internet and questionable material in books, magazines and electronic media. And we don't have forty years to instill the Word of God in our children's hearts. We must determine to find ways early in their lives to teach scriptural truths and disciplines.

Your selection of this book reveals that you take Jesus' words seriously when He said, "Let the little children come to me" (Mark 10:14). You understand that if a child comes to know Jesus when he is still trusting and innocent, the greater the chances that he will decide to follow Christ as an adult. Who is better qualified to lead little ones to Christ but their own parents?

Susanna Wesley, mother of John and Charles Wesley, understood the importance of guiding her nineteen children to the Lord at an early age. Susanna once wrote, "the children were always put into a regular method of living . . . from their birth."[1] Her idea of "regular method of living" included devotional and prayer time every morning.

Like Susanna, you may want to make certain your children lead disciplined lives, but your time is limited. The mother of the Wesleys said, "I have lived such a retired life for so many years, used to employ my time and care in bringing up my children. No one can, without renouncing the world in the most literal sense, observe my method; and there are few, if any, that would entirely devote twenty years of prime life in hopes to save the souls of their children."[2]

Susanna was right. How many of us can or would devote the hours she did solely on our children? Our lives today are too complicated and full of other "important" things. We can weave, however, the same ideas and disciplines into our daily lives. Our sons or daughters may not write history-changing sermons or hymns, but we can lead them into a deeper walk with God. We may not know God's plan for our children, but we can encourage them to seek His will while they are young.

This book strives to follow the message of Deuteronomy 6:4-9 and Mark 12:30. Several chapters provide ideas for teaching children how to love God with all their heart, mind, soul and strength through spiritual disciplines.

Our goal as Christian parents should be to touch our children's lives so that they will "set apart Christ as Lord" in their hearts (1 Peter 3:15). Though each child develops his or her own personality, each age group has certain common characteristics. Understanding these behavior patterns can help you point your children toward applying spiritual discipline in their lives.

Jesus added one element to the commandment written in Deuteronomy when He said to love the Lord with all your *mind* as well as your heart, soul and strength (Mark 12:30; Luke 10:27). By filling a child's mind with the things of God, we stand a better chance of reaching his heart. Instilling habits of spiritual disciplines can help turn a child's thoughts toward God.

God has placed a purpose in each child's life. Some Bible versions use the word "might" instead of strength, which denotes effort and control. By understanding a child's physical strengths and abilities as well as his emotional strengths, such as willpower and motivation, parents can help a child understand God's plan. Through teaching spiritual discipline we can encourage our children to develop the talents God has placed in them.

You may be able to fill your child's mind with Bible stories and even steer his heart somewhat, but his soul belongs to God: "For every living soul belongs to me" (Ezekiel 18:4). Only our prayers and guidance can have an effect on our children's souls. I have heard it said that a mother's prayers unlock the gates of heaven for her children. Yet in times of struggle or frustration, the words don't come easily. This book will give you suggestions on how to pray for and guide your children's lives.

Jesus told us in Matthew 7:13-14, "Enter through the narrow gate. For wide is the gate and broad is the road that leads to destruction, and many enter through it. But small is the gate and narrow the road that leads to life, and only a few find it." The closing sections of each chapter, entitled *The Narrow Path*, offer Bible readings, thoughts, questions and prayers for parents to meditate on during their personal devotional times. As we "walk along the way" with our children, we want to make certain that we stay on the narrow path by practicing the spiritual disciplines in our own lives.

As You Walk Along the Way: How to Lead Your Child on the Path of Spiritual Discipline flows from the heart of one parent to another. It's the result of over twenty-five years of my joy, tears and hopes as a parent. I will share ideas my husband and I found effective in raising our three sons and many temporary custody children. Stories of failures as well as triumphs are meant to help you realize that you are not alone. This book does not promise to have all the answers. My children continually remind me that I'm not so smart. But I do hope that I can spur you on to find new ideas of your own.

As the Lord writes His commandments on your heart, it is my hope that this book gives you wonderful things to talk about when you arise and when you lie down, when you sit at home and as you walk along the way. But most of all, my prayer is that you will hold your children on your lap and teach them to love Jesus.

The Narrow Path

Scripture reading: Matthew 16:24

Spiritual Guides

There is a more excellent way, but it is too narrow to admit the trailing garments of passionate desire, too narrow for pride, self-indulgence, greed and avarice—it is the Way of the Cross, but it leads to Life! (F.B. Meyer, *Our Daily Walk*)

Light on the Path

Let us fix our eyes on Jesus, the author and perfecter of our faith, who for the joy set before him endured the cross, scorning its shame, and sat down at the right hand of the throne of God. (Hebrews 12:2)

1. As you begin to walk the narrow path, what things or activities tend to take your eyes off Jesus?
2. Name the crosses in your life that you must endure.
3. Describe the joy set before you.

Your Traveling Companion

In sincerity and humility, tell God, *Show me where I have slipped off the narrow path.*

Chapter Two

DISCOVERING THE SPIRITUAL DISCIPLINES

Parenthood reminds me of farming. Having had many farmers in my family, I understand the hard work it takes to prepare the soil for the seed in order to reap a harvest. A farmer doesn't just plow the ground—he plants, waters, feeds and pulls weeds. When his labor is finished, the farmer can enjoy his crop.

> When a farmer plows for planting, does he plow continually?
>   Does he keep on breaking up and harrowing the soil?
> When he has leveled the surface,
>   does he not sow caraway and scatter cummin?
> Does he not plant wheat in its place,
>   barleys in its plot,
>   and spelt in its field?
> His God instructs him
>   and teaches him the right way. (Isaiah 28:24-26)

Our children's hearts and minds are like soil waiting for God's Word to be planted in them. As parents we must break up the ground, plant the seeds, water and feed our children if we hope to reap a harvest of righteousness. I'm afraid sometimes we have a tendency to plow continually. We nag and prod and coax our children to qualities we think they should have. Yet, God has a plan on how to form the personalities and talents in our children. Like the farmer in the above passage, God instructs and teaches parents "the right way." Just as the farmer uses tools to tend his fields, God gives us tools to care for the hearts of our children. Those tools are spiritual disciplines such as prayer, confession and worship.

Knowing my family, I'm sure parenting didn't come easy for Granny. Yet I don't believe she sat down and made a plan to teach her grandchildren. It came naturally. Likewise, Tim and I never really planned to train our children how to pray, worship or confess sins. It resulted from wanting each child to "Love the Lord their God with all their heart, soul, mind and strength." Practicing the spiritual disciplines begins with a longing to know God and surrendering all to Him. The term *discipline* itself is one we often avoid. It denotes breaking, conforming and training that we may not want to experience. The spiritual disciplines, however, are a gift from God that leads to inner righteousness. "No discipline seems pleasant at the time, but painful. Later on, however, it produces a harvest of righteousness and peace for those who have been trained by it" (Hebrews 12:11).

Although Granny started me on the road to a life of journaling and love for God's Word, I have found it hard at times to be consistent in my devotional life. There were times I struggled to get time alone with God. As an adult trying to renew my relationship with the Lord, I tried all the "quiet time" tricks. I had an elaborate notebook system with prayer lists and journal pages. I went through the steps of thanksgiving, adoration and praise to ease the guilt of constantly laying my requests before God. All this left me empty and dry. Becoming a parent helped me desire more than rituals and legalism. I wanted more for my children. I wanted them to have a *relationship* with God apart from me or their father.

Without a desire to obey the greatest commandment to love God and a longing for our children to do the same, practices such as meditation, fasting or study become the kind of outward methods Paul discussed in Colossians 2:20-23:

> Since you died with Christ to the basic principles of this world, why, as though you still belonged to it, do you submit to its rules: "Do not handle! Do not taste! Do not touch!"? These are all destined to perish with use, because they are based on human commands and teachings. Such regulations indeed have an appearance of wisdom, with their self-imposed worship, their false humility and their harsh treatment of the body, but they lack any value in restraining sensual indulgence.

Childlike Faith

Jesus understood that children play an important part in the faith community. Children are totally dependent upon a power greater than themselves and Jesus said that we, as adults, must obtain this childlike faith.

> He called a little child and had him stand among them. And he said: "I tell you the truth, unless you change and be-come like little children, you will never enter the kingdom of heaven. Therefore, whoever humbles himself like this child is the greatest in the kingdom of heaven.
> "And whoever welcomes a little child like this in my name welcomes me." (Matthew 18:2-5)

I first began to truly understand this concept of having childlike faith when my children were very young. As they relied on those clos-est to them, namely my husband and myself, they developed trust. Once they learned that people and events are not always trustworthy, they needed to develop faith. Christianity provides an answer for the contradictory aspects of life a child will encounter. This is the kind of faith Jesus spoke of in the above passage—a faith that accepts the negatives and the positives of life.

The church I grew up in didn't believe that God intervened directly in our lives. "God only helps those who help themselves" was the motto. I was told that God spoke from the skies to the prophets of old, but not to us today. At a very young age, this all seemed quite contradictory to me. Since Jesus said that we could cry "Abba, Abba," I questioned this. *Why would a God who didn't guide us every moment of every day want to be called "Da Da?"* As I grew older and found myself caught in the struggle to be "good enough," my childlike faith began to fade. Watching the simple faith of my children helped me to regain the same trust in my own life.

How do we encourage this faith, or as Deuteronomy says, to "impress" the commandments of God on our children? Learning is the lifelong process of acquiring skills, knowledge and behavior through experience. Through the process of discovery and repetition a child learns to filter routine stimuli from new, important information. Our children are more likely to grow up having lifelong relationships with God if we instill spiritual disciplines before they reach their teen years.

In the chapters that follow, we will look closely at how we can encourage our children to have spiritual discipline in their lives. Tim and I practiced the disciplines in our lives and with our children, but it wasn't until I read Richard Foster's classic, *Celebration of Discipline* (revised edition), that I had a name for what we were doing. Up until then we just referred to the disciplines by their names, such as fasting, prayer or confession. We knew we wanted to deal with sin and have lives controlled by the Spirit. Obeying the Scriptures by practicing the disciplines reminded us that "God did not give us a spirit of timidity, but a spirit of power, of love and of self-discipline" (2 Timothy 1:7).

Even after practicing the spiritual disciplines for many years, I am still learning how to explore the inward life through disciplines like contemplative prayer, solitude and simplicity. I have discovered, however, that teaching children the disciplines draws them into an intimate relationship with God. I borrowed the list of disciplines from Richard Foster, since it is the most complete list I have found. Some of them are familiar. Others you may have never established in your own life, much less your child's. All the disciplines press on the whole of the child. I hope to show you how particular disciplines can guide and affect the heart, soul, mind or strength of your child.

Prayer

The disciples asked Jesus, "Lord, teach us to pray" (Luke 11:1). Prayer is learned. The disciples had prayed in the synagogues all their lives. So why did they feel the need to be taught? The answer is simple—they were learning by Jesus' example that prayer had an effect on the world around them. They watched as Jesus went off to solitary places to pray then returned to heal the sick. They stood in amazement as He thanked God and then fed 5,000 people with just a few loaves of bread and a couple of fish. The modern sentiment, "prayer changes things," was real to them.

While this is probably the most familiar of the spiritual disciplines, most of us have felt lost as to what to say in prayer. Therefore it's encouraging to remember that prayer is a learned process. Throughout this book, I will share specific ways to teach children to pray. Poetry prayers such as "Now I lay me down to sleep" are sweet and comforting, but we want our children to know that prayer is natural conversation with their heavenly Father. As we learn to pray in deeper ways, our children will learn along with us.

Worship

Worship is more than fulfilling the commandment to love God with all your heart, soul and mind. It's a response to God loving us. It is being deeply aware of the presence of the Father, inside and outside a church building. When our youngest son, Josiah, was in kindergarten, we left the house for school one day in a hurry. As a result, we had missed our daily quiet time of prayer and worship. On the way to school Josiah spoke up. "Mommy, I think we forgot to take Jesus with us."

The key to worshiping God is to acknowledge His presence in all things. Brother Lawrence wrote, "We should stop for a few minutes as often as possible to praise God from the depths of our hearts, to enjoy Him there in secret." Josiah felt the lack of God's presence because we had cultivated the habit of daily worship. We stopped in the parking lot, forgetting about our tardiness, and asked Jesus to go to school with Josiah.

Study

How do we teach children to love God with all their minds? The spiritual discipline of study trains the mind to think and move in a certain direction. Our central passage in Deuteronomy instructs parents to write God's laws on their gates and their door frames (6:9).

Study involves repetition and exposure to an idea. Granny's "panty hose Scriptures" helped me to memorize favorite passages from the Bible. From the time Joshua was six months old, we had a daily quiet time. At this stage the word discipline took on a whole new meaning in my life. It took hard work and determination to make sure that each child had a daily quiet time. Mark was six and starting to have more independent quiet times while Joshua and I read Bible stories and sang songs. Joshua learned to count by naming the days of Creation. The story of Creation also became the basis for learning colors and animal names.

Since quiet times were part of the daily routine, Josiah joined in at birth, sitting in an infant carrier while his brother recited the books of the Bible and raised his hands in praise. Before he was a year old, Josiah surprisingly announced that "the Bible has two pots—The Old Tetament and the New Tetament." I wasn't starry-eyed enough to think that my toddler understood what he was parroting, but I was excited that repetition was having an impact. From there we could build on the familiar and instill a love and understanding of God's Word.

Meditation

Unfortunately, Christian meditation has been greatly misunderstood due to prevalent Eastern religious practices. In reality, the two are not at all alike. Richard Foster identifies the distinction: "Eastern meditation is an attempt to empty the mind; Christian meditation is an attempt to fill the mind. The two ideas are quite different."[1] Foster explains that Eastern meditation encourages *detachment* from the world in order to make room for the cosmic forces. Christian meditation, however, encourages detachment from the *confusion* of the world in order that we might gain *attachment* to God.

How do we teach children to meditate? Certainly not by sitting in a lotus position and chanting, "Ommm"! But we can encourage our children to spend time thinking about God. For example, when our children were elementary age and into middle school, we encouraged a time of meditation when they came home from school. After hugs and kisses and the news of the day, they retreated to their rooms or a private place to "shake off" the world and meditate on God. In only ten or twenty minutes, they came out refreshed and ready to serve and love the family. It also gave me time to regroup for an evening of homework, chores, dinner, baths and bedtime stories.

We had been practicing this for several years when one day I read Acts 3:1: "Peter and John were going up to the temple at the time of prayer—at 3 in the afternoon." Imagine my excitement to find out that the time of prayer was at "three in the afternoon"—the very time my children came home from school and retreated to their time of meditation and prayer!

Solitude

There is a big difference between being *alone* and solitude. When we were first married, my in-laws warned me that Tim "liked being alone." Apparently, he had spent many hours of his teen life in his room or camping by himself. Being a "people person" myself, who had spent most of her free time doing community service work, this was a scary thing.

But as I grew to know my husband better, I realized that Tim had found a secret in his solitude—the same mystery that Thomas à Kempis knew. He wrote, "In silence and in stillness a religious soul advances himself and learns the mysteries of the Holy Scripture. Whoever, therefore, withdraws himself from his acquaintances and friends, God will draw near unto him with His holy angels."[2]

I can still remember the cozy corner that Granny sent me to for "down time." I would curl up with a book or write in my journal. As my life got busier I began to forget how much solitude drew me closer to God. We can meditate and pray sometimes with others around, but there are those times when we need to draw away and hear God say, "Be still, and know that I am God" (Psalm 46:10).

Fortunately, Tim has always kept that in check for the entire family. For example, one day when Joshua was about ten he asked to go for a bike ride. I quickly said, "No, dinner is almost ready." Tim interceded and told me that dinner could wait. It had been an even busier than normal day and Joshua needed some solitude. Years later, after he had been driving for awhile, Joshua shared with me his secret "prayer closets" in the mountains and out on the prairies, near our Colorado home.

Fasting

This is probably one of the hardest yet most rewarding of the spiritual disciplines. You're probably thinking, *Make a child fast? I find it hard enough to fast myself!* I had the same thought. But then I read, "Blow the trumpet in Zion, declare a holy fast, call a sacred assembly. Gather the people, consecrate the assembly; bring together the elders, gather the children, those nursing at the breast" (Joel 2:15-16).

Fasting as viewed in Scripture is the abstaining from food for spiritual purposes. Often it refers to a partial fast, as when Daniel ate no meat and drank no wine for three weeks (Daniel 10:3). This is the type of fast our children participated in when they were really small. As they grew older, we allowed them to decide how much abstinence they felt God was calling them to.

Fasting doesn't just have to be abstaining from food. We have often taken fasts from television or other activities for the purpose of spending extra time with God. Fasting leads to more self-control in everyday life. When Tim and I are away from the house, our teens will call us on the cell phone to ask permission before watching a video or television show. What amazes us is that we never actually laid down a rule for our kids to do this; it flowed from a life of discipline.

Confession

When our oldest son was eighteen he announced, "God is just not enough. He may be enough for you, but He's not for me!" My husband and I watched him walk out of our lives to "find himself." For months following that day, I wrestled with thoughts of failure as a mother. *What had I done wrong? Wasn't the main goal in our children's lives to make "God enough"—above all else the world had to offer?* I pondered over the mistakes I knew I had made—ignoring little lies and acts of selfishness, giving in when God wasn't enough.

When our middle son reached eighteen he began making plans to enter into ministry. Looking back, I realize that Tim and I haven't raised our middle boy much differently than our eldest. But there is one major distinction between my two sons—confession. When confronted with sin or temptation our oldest son always chose to deny any struggle. On the other hand, our middle son readily and voluntarily admits the things he contends with. He has learned the truth found in James 5:16: "Therefore confess your sins to each other and pray for each other so that you may be healed."

Confession is part of the redemptive process. "Without the cross, the discipline of confession would be only psychologically therapeutic. But it is so much more. It involves an objective change in our relationship with God and a subjective change in us. It is a means of healing and transforming the inner spirit."[3]

We don't often think of confession as a spiritual discipline. But it is something that has to be learned and taught. It's not easy to "bear one's soul" to another. Parents must set the example by confessing their sins and errors to their children. Later I will show that through gentle, yet sometimes firm reasoning, a child's heart and motives can be brought into the light. A household full of truth and honesty draws a family closer to God as well as each other. "But if we walk in the light, as he is in the light, we have fellowship with one another, and the blood of Jesus, his Son, purifies us from all sin" (1 John 1:7).

Guidance

In the middle of the day, Tim answered the phone. On the other end was the voice of a very frustrated teacher. It seemed she had given her second grade class a writing assignment and Joshua refused to participate. "All I asked them to do is start their papers with *I wish* . . . and then write what they wanted!" making her irritation with our son quite clear.

Tim silently laughed and asked, "Did he give you a reason?"

She said, "He says he never wishes, but always asks God for direction."

"Well," my husband replied calmly, "what if Joshua starts his paper with *I pray* . . .? Would that work?"

The teacher consented and my husband hung up, delighted that our son had learned that the Lord guided him in all things. Our job as parents is to guide our children in such a way that they grow up to be responsible adults. A child that cannot make decisions apart from his parents becomes a frustrated, insecure adult. We should want our children to grow out of the relationship of parent and child to one of brothers and sisters in Christ, "because those who are led by the Spirit of God are sons of God" (Romans 8:14). The spiritual discipline of guidance allows our children to move from being guided by their parents to being led by the Spirit.

Service

In our home, my children have witnessed the act of serving others. We have had more than forty adults and twenty-five children share our home. Learning to "lay down" their lives wasn't a choice; it was a necessity. Service with a smile, however, was something our children had to choose to practice. It was not always an easy choice.

We can teach our children to serve in little ways, such as doing chores, helping a neighbor or taking care of a pet. There is, however, more to the discipline of service than *acting* like a servant. We must teach our children to *become* servants. Scriptures such as, "Greater love has no one than this, that he lay down his life for his friends" (John 15:13) or "If anyone wants to be first, he must be the very last, and the servant of all" (Mark 9:35) must become our guide in serving others.

Children learn to serve by example. I recall Granny's door always being opened to others. I remember helping her in the kitchen preparing meals for church or a family in need. I have fond memories of her father, Grandpa Ray, even though he died when I was seven. Many people have told me over the years how he gave them "the shirt off his back." In the chapter on loving God with all our strength, we will discuss how to teach our children the discipline of service. For now, let us realize that service is a spiritual discipline that we must demonstrate and cultivate in our children's lives.

Submission

If you've been a parent for very long you know the heartbreak and frustration of a disobedient child. No matter how much we might struggle with disciplining our children, we want them to obey us because we know it is the right thing to do.

> Children, obey your parents in the Lord, for this is right. "Honor your father and mother"—which is the first commandment with a promise—"that it may go well with you

and that you may enjoy long life on the earth." (Ephesians
6:1-3)

The practice of the discipline of submission goes beyond obedience;
it is a willful decision of the heart to deny what we want in order to submit to someone else. We can mold our children into being obedient, but
their hearts may grow to resent following our commands. Jesus' teachings centered around the denial of self. His whole life was one of
self-denial. Practicing the discipline of submission begins with obeying His command found in Mark 8:34-35: "If anyone would come after
me, he must deny himself and take up his cross and follow me. For
whoever wants to save his life will lose it, but whoever loses his life for
me and for the gospel will save it."

Simplicity

Of all the disciplines, simplicity is probably my weakest area. When
we packed up our home of over thirteen years and moved across the
country, I felt the meaning of the verse, ". . . the abundance of a rich
man permits him no sleep" (Ecclesiastes 5:12). As we collected our unwanted possessions for a garage sale, I was amazed at how much we
had accumulated over the years. Tim and I have had someone living
with us twenty-two out of the twenty-five years of our marriage. Bat-
tered wives and their children, college students, families, teens and single men and women have found shelter in our home—which meant the
extra beds and dressers, silverware and dishes, clothing and just plain
"stuff." And since much of our ministry centered around computers,
we had enough outdated parts for a small electronics store. In the
frenzy of sorting and packing all that "stuff," there was a realization
that God had certainly more than abundantly provided for all our
needs.

When I think of simplicity, I think of purity. When our motives are
sifted and refined we want to simplify our lives. The spiritual discipline of simplicity starts with inner contentment, which means we have
pure motives for all we say and do. Although we collected many

things, I think I can honestly say we used almost everything for the Lord. There were many times when we had no groceries, but the needs of the ministry always came first. Striving to teach our children purity of heart helped them to join with the apostle Paul in confessing, "I know what it is to be in need, and I know what it is to have plenty. I have learned the secret of being content in any and every situation, whether well fed or hungry, whether living in plenty or in want" (Philippians 4:12).

Celebration

As a little tyke, Josiah seemed to grumble a lot. He struggled with being content and always wanted his way. (As a preschooler, he announced plans to live with some friends because they had a hot tub!) I became determined that my youngest son would overcome this ill temperament. Every morning when he woke up I would say, "Morning, Sunshine! This is the day that the Lord has made. And you *will* rejoice." Under my breath I would add, "Whether you like it or not."

Now a teenager, Josiah still doesn't smile as much as I would like. (I try to give him the benefit of the doubt, because he wears braces.) But as he has grown in obedience to us and to the Lord, he has gained a joy that can only come from God. Celebration is the spiritual discipline that gives strength to all the other disciplines. All the other disciplines should be filled with thanksgiving and celebration. Without joy, we grow tired and our obedience grows weak. As Nehemiah declared, "the joy of the LORD is your strength" (Nehemiah 8:10).

Remember, our goal is for our children to love the Lord with all their hearts, souls, minds and strength. The spiritual disciplines are the catalysts that cause this reaction in their hearts. As parents we must realize that we cannot make children gain inner transformation through sheer human willpower and discipline. Inner righteousness is a gift from God and only He can work from the inside out. God has given parents, however, the special task of raising children in Him. We are the farmers plowing the ground and the spiritual disciplines are our tools.

The Narrow Path

Scripture reading: Proverbs 1:7

Spiritual Guides

Whence then does the true fear of God arise? From the knowledge of our own sinfulness and a sense of the presence of God. (A.W. Tozer, *The Root of the Righteous*)

Light on the Path

Fear God and keep his commandments, for this is the whole duty of man. (Ecclesiastes 12:13)

He who heeds discipline shows the way to life, but whoever ignores correction leads others astray. (Proverbs 10:17)

1. How have you feared God before? In what ways should you fear Him?
2. What areas of your life lack discipline? How has this affected your children or others?
3. Which of the spiritual disciplines do you long to improve or add to your life?

Your Traveling Companion

Ask God, *Place a holy fear for You in my heart, which will help me to practice discipline in my life and keep your commandments.*

Chapter Three

DOING AND BEING

I stood in my kitchen fuming and slamming pots and pans, totally frustrated because I felt like Martha again (Luke 10:38-42). I knew I had no business feeling this way. But like Paul when he wrote to the Roman church, I struggled with what I knew I should do and what I actually did (Romans 7:18-21).

So there I was fussing that I was left alone to prepare a meal for an "army." The thoughts began to churn in my head. *Martha got a bum rap! Hey, Jesus was the Son of God and she just wanted to give Him a decent meal.*

Like Martha, I often scurry around the house making life miserable for everyone in my path. For years, the number at our table has been as high as eighteen or twenty; it is seldom less than twelve. I know exactly how Martha must have felt when Jesus and His disciples stopped by unexpectedly. Martha counted on her sister Mary to help with the preparations. And on this particular night I didn't want to be left alone in the kitchen either!

People often drop by our house. Much of the time, however, I'm not included in the "adult conversation" because I must prepare the meal, help kids with homework or solve a minor crisis or two. Sure, I had a couple of kids helping me, but I still thought it was unfair that the other adults weren't pitching in. So my foul mood grew deeper and as soon as one of the kids made a mistake, I snapped.

Before I said something I would regret, I ran back to my room and plopped on the bed. I wanted to hide, because I knew that if Tim saw me he would say for the hundredth time, "Carla, Carla, you are upset about many things." Warm tears began to stream down my face.

"Lord, why doesn't anyone understand how much I have to do around here?"

As the words came out of my mouth, they tasted bitter and selfish. My particular "Mary" at the time was a young woman dealing with some real problems in her life. She and her son were spending a lot of time at our house, while she received counseling from my husband.

Oh God, I'm jealous! I cried in my heart. For the first time, I realized that Martha's sin was jealousy. She deserved Jesus' rebuke and I did, too. I wiped my tears and got down on my knees. *Lord, forgive my jealousy. Please help me to rest in You.* I remained there for a time, allowing God's forgiveness and quietness to fill my heart and mind.

When I returned to the kitchen, I could see the worried expressions on my children's faces. I realized how my actions had affected them. I asked them for forgiveness and we joyfully prepared the meal. But their little faces remained on my mind. If my goal was to teach them to love God with all their heart, soul, mind and strength, my actions certainly didn't show it.

I share my "Martha" story for two reasons: first, to demonstrate how our behavior affects our children, who are always watching us; and second, to confess that, in looking for ways to instill the spiritual disciplines in our children's lives, we can begin to feel overwhelmed.

I imagine your life feels full already and the thought of adding something more to your plate makes you shudder. One time a friend challenged me to take a paper plate and write every commitment I had on it. There wasn't a millimeter of space left when I finished. As I examined my plate, I couldn't see anything that I could drop—except maybe obedience school with my dog! I lifted my plate up to God and gave it all to

Him, asking Him to show me how to remain in His presence in the midst of all those things.

Of course, children-related activities took up much of the space on my plate, so I realized that teaching my children to love God with all their hearts wasn't something I had to *add* to my plate. Every commitment in my life, even those that didn't directly involve my children, must play a part in leading them to the Lord. The closer I came to God, the better example my children would have to follow.

I've learned that there is a happy balance between Martha and Mary. In her book *Living a Purpose-Full Life*, Jan Johnson describes the differences between *doing* and *being*. She says, "Separating the inner spiritual life from outward purposes leads to frustration"[1]—the type of frustration I felt that day in my kitchen. Because I was so caught up in *doing*, I had detached myself from just *being* in God's presence and opened the door to jealousy and bitterness. My family and guests certainly needed to eat, but in peaceful surroundings. As Proverbs says, "Better a meal of vegetables where there is love than a fattened calf with hatred" (Proverbs 15:17). I needed to find the balance between Mary and Martha.

Deuteronomy 6:7 tells us that we are to teach our children to love the Lord "when you sit at home and when you walk along the road." This book will suggest a lot of things to *do* with your children to encourage them to love God. Teaching your children spiritual disciplines helps them to *be* with God. The doing and the being will weave together so that whatever your children do in word or deed they will do it for the glory of God (1 Corinthians 10:31).

With All Your Heart

Early in our marriage Tim and I made a commitment to obey the following passages:

> The man who loves his life will lose it, while the man who hates his life in this world will keep it for eternal life. (John 12:25)

> If anyone comes to me and does not hate his father and
> mother, his wife and children, his brothers and sisters—yes,
> even his own life—he cannot be my disciple. (Luke 14:26)

Jesus continually found different ways to say we must love the Lord
with all our heart, mind, soul and strength. The above Scriptures were
just another way for Jesus to tell His disciples *how* to obey the greatest
commandment. In my husband's book, *The Essential Piece: Living
Luke 14:26 in Everyday Life,* Tim says:

> We must love God with *all*. All means 100 percent! How-
> ever, to those who say that Luke 14:26 and John 12:25 means
> only that we love God more than all other things, all means
> only 51 percent. They love God more than all other loves,
> therefore, they allow a small majority to suffice. . . . The
> greatest commandment does not read, "Love the Lord your
> God with a majority of your mind, strength and soul." The
> commandment says all, which means 100 percent."[2]

As Tim and I began to live this out we knew we wanted our children
to do the same. My husband hadn't been raised in the church, but I had.
I didn't want my children growing up like me and discovering that
their relationship with the Lord was shallow and empty, with no clue of
how to practice the spiritual disciplines. My youthful prayers had been
selfish and centered on what God could do for me. My evangelical up-
bringing had made Bible study "ink" written "on tablets of stone" (2
Corinthians 3:3) instead of written on my heart. Worship was predictable—two songs (first, second and last stanzas) and a prayer. Meditation was something my friends did at school, and I knew I would be
grounded if I tried it myself. Fasting was what Gandhi practiced and
solitude meant a good soak in the bathtub.

I argued in my heart and with my parents and church leaders that
there had to be more to being a Christian, but my questioning was often
misunderstood for rebellion.

Finally, I did rebel and for a short time tried to fill the void with drugs, alcohol and sex. But when you know in your heart that you are the "temple of the Holy Spirit" (1 Corinthians 6:19), you can't run for long. Becoming pregnant out of wedlock became a welcome detour on the road to destruction. Although Tim had been raised with little or no religious background, he at least had a longing to know God.

So as we began our journey to draw close to the Lord, Tim and I soon realized that nothing could stand between us and God—not even each other. We wanted to love God with *all* our hearts and for our children to do the same. Taking a closer look at Deuteronomy 6:5-9 shows how the spiritual disciplines flow from that desire:

> Love the LORD your God with all your heart and with all your soul and with all your strength. These commandments that I give you today are to be upon your hearts. Impress them on your children. Talk about them when you sit at home and when you walk along the road, when you lie down and when you get up. Tie them as symbols on your hands and bind them on your foreheads. Write them on the doorframes of your houses and on your gates.

God is a jealous God and longs for complete attention and adoration. The Lord told the Israelites—the same goes for us today—that His commandments are to be upon our hearts. I don't believe that God was limiting this to the Ten Commandments. While that's a good place to start, He wants us to love and obey His entire Word. But just reading the Bible doesn't mean that His commandments are on our hearts. It is through obedience that God's law becomes part of us. As the Psalmist wrote:

> Blessed are they whose ways are blameless,
>   who walk according to the law of the LORD.
> Blessed are they who keep his statutes
>   and seek him with all their heart.

They do nothing wrong;
    they walk in his ways.
You have laid down precepts
    that are to be fully obeyed.
        (Psalm 119:1-4)

Before we can "impress" God's commandments on our children, we must obey them ourselves. Psalm 119:1 says, "Blessed are those whose ways are blameless." Walking according to God's law makes our hearts above reproach. David was a man after God's own heart because he did what God asked him to do (Acts 13:22). Yet David committed such sins as adultery and murder, two from the "top ten list." That doesn't seem "blameless" to me. But the key in David's life was that he was a man who loved God with all his heart. Therefore when he did sin, he fully confessed it.

Confession is the starting point of having God's commandments on our hearts. By confessing our sins to each other and being honest about our struggles and temptations, we walk according to God's law and therefore can be found blameless. As First John 1:9 says, "If we confess our sins, he is faithful and just and will forgive us our sins and purify us from all unrighteousness." Through confession we forgive one another and remind each other that Jesus' blood cleanses us from our sins. Therefore, being honest with our children is also the starting point of impressing God's commandments on their hearts.

When our oldest, Mark, turned nine we realized that we needed to tell him about how he came into the world outside of God's perfect order. We wanted him to hear the truth from us before he heard it from someone else. After we confessed our sin to our son he asked, "How could you have hurt God like that?" Of course, at the time, his comment broke our hearts. Years later, however, Mark happened to walk by while I was having a conversation with a young woman who struggled with a serious mistake she had made. My son, then fifteen, piped in and said, "God works through mistakes! I'm one!" Our son felt our love and God's through openness, honesty and confession of sin.

Confessing our sins to each other means that we also help each other see our sins clearly. As the Apostle Paul wrote, "Instead, speaking the truth in love, we will in all things grow up into him who is the Head, that is, Christ" (Ephesians 4:15). This goes for our children as well. In order to help them to love God with all their hearts, we must first help our children to see the areas in which they do not love God.

Children have a really narrow view of the world, especially when it comes to something they do wrong. Their limited years of experience keep them from seeing their choices as wrong. Tim and I have discovered that the secret to helping a child see his heart clearly is through gentle, yet firm, reasoning. I have to admit that Tim is better at this than I am. I would rather just tell them the answers than take the time to draw thoughts out of my children, but that is not how God, our Parent, operates.

In Isaiah 1:18 the Lord tells Israel, "Come now, let us reason together. . . . Though your sins are like scarlet, they shall be as white as snow." He then explains the consequences of sin and the rewards of obedience. God reasoned with His people and drew them into a relationship with Him. We can do the same thing with our children, whether they are stubborn two-year-olds or twelve-year-olds who think they can out-reason us.

Through reasoning we help our children to see their motives clearly. Asking questions instead of just handing down verdicts helps a child discover truths on his own. When a child discovers the answers for himself, he's more likely to apply the information. A classic example of a common power struggle between parent and child is homework. It is a rare child indeed who chooses to do homework over playing outside or watching television. Asking questions like, "How much time do you need?" or "What would be good choices for you in order to complete your homework?" helps a child discover that doing his homework eases family tension and allows more time to play. It certainly works much better than saying, "Why don't you ever do your homework?" or "You won't watch television for five years if you don't do your homework!"

Reasoning doesn't just work with infractions of the law. It also helps a child understand God's law. Leading a child through a thinking process reveals the meaning behind God's Word. I think this is what God meant when He said to "impress them on your children." For example, a twelve-year-old boy who lived with us for about a year had a hard time with the concept of hell. Jason would often make comments that revealed his struggles with the possibility of people he loved perishing. Often Tim would steer the conversation in a direction that helped the boy think and reason about this concept. Tim might ask, "What if someone came into your home and tormented your brother or mother? How would you feel if the person were never punished?" This caused Jason to consider God's justice and fairness. Tim also shared passages like Second Peter 3:9: "The Lord is not slow in keeping his promise, as some understand slowness. He is patient with you, not wanting anyone to perish, but everyone to come to repentance."

Remember to reason with your child at his level of capability. Don't give him more information than he can handle. Jason never asked, "Why doesn't God just destroy all bad people instead of sending them to hell?" so Tim never tried to answer that. He never went beyond what he felt the boy could reason out. A child's ability to reason is directly related to his ability to understand language. He may not be able to express a clear response, but he may understand what was asked of him. Learning to reason with your child as you sit and walk along the way will point him to a personal relationship with the Lord.

As I said before, I am not as good at reasoning as my husband; though I want to give our children the answers and solutions to problems, I often have to depend on Tim to guide our children through the thinking process. This is a difficult problem for many single parents. Often in our ministry a frazzled mother will call Tim or me because her child has boxed her into a corner and she needs help. Single mothers and fathers need the support of Christian brothers and sisters. Children without fathers need guidance and an authority figure. Those without mothers need comforting and understanding. If you are a single parent, you still need to teach your child to love God with all his heart, but you need help. Families with both the father and mother need to bring single parent families along with them as they walk along the way.

God laid down some explicit instructions as to when to impress His laws on the hearts of our children. He could have said, "Love the Lord your God with all your heart, all day long." Instead He gave a detailed list of when to teach our children God's Word. In the following chapters we will look at how to teach the specific spiritual disciplines to our children, but here are some suggestions for teaching God's Word that might fall under the instructions in Deuteronomy:

As you sit at home

❤ Meal times provide some of the best opportunities for discussions. Sometimes, for example, it is apparent that a child has done something he shouldn't because he is so quiet at the table. Just one word can open up an entire discussion.

❤ Provide plenty of board games, puzzles and toys that will keep children occupied at home. In our culture, families have so many activities that take them in so many directions. Spend time playing with your children, looking for "teachable moments" to share God's truths.

❤ Change worldly toys into ones that point children to the Lord. Since Barbie® dolls encouraged characteristics we didn't find acceptable in our home, I looked for replacements for this much-desired toy. I purchased several sets of nine-inch dolls and a friend made Bible-era clothing for them. These were a big hit, as the kids made the dolls go through stories such as Joseph or Queen Esther.

❤ Allow your child to sit and talk with you while you prepare meals or do other chores. Jason often sat in Tim's office reading or drawing without even talking. They enjoyed each other's silent company, which helped the boy feel secure to ask questions at other times.

♥ Fill your shelves with books that retell the wonderful stories of the Bible. Read these books into a tape recorder so that your children can listen to them whenever they want.

As you walk along the road

In our culture this might read "as you drive down the road." We spend a lot of time in our cars. Use these times to start conversations with your children about God's Word.

♥ Leave Scripture cards in the glove compartment of your car. Pull them out and have your child read one and discuss its meaning.

♥ Sing songs with little ones still in car seats that point their thoughts toward the Lord.

♥ Take walks as a family. We have had some wonderful discussions during leisurely ten-minute walks. In our house we could have as many as six or seven children. Tim and I would take turns taking individual kids on walks for "you and me" time.

♥ Longer road trips allow time for longer discussions. Our children always knew they could debate respectfully with us. Tim often initiates and steers discussion to make them think about subjects such as evolution, Eastern religions or abortion, depending on the age level of the kids in the car. Discussing such subjects beforehand prepares children to give answers from their own hearts to friends and teachers.

When you lie down and when you get up

♥ Set a time limit when homework and baths should be completed. This frees you to spend time talking with your children before bedtime. A rushed child goes to bed with the thoughts of the world on his mind, instead of the things of the Lord.

❤ When the boys were little I sent them to their dad for a kiss goodnight and I tucked them in with a bedtime story and prayer. But as they reached elementary school age, Tim took over this job. Bedtime stories were replaced with discussions with their dad about their day and how to apply God's Word in certain situations.

❤ Have your children lay out their clothes for the next day before going to bed. Remind them that Jesus said we were to be "dressed and ready for service" (Luke 12:35).

❤ Teach your children to think of the Lord before hopping out of bed. I started this very young by taking my boys out of the crib with "This is the day the Lord has made."

❤ We will talk more about this later, but start every day with a quiet time. When the boys were really little, we had quiet time right after breakfast. But by elementary school age, they could deny themselves long enough for a quiet time before they ate. This taught them to "seek first his kingdom and his righteousness" (Matthew 6:33).

Tie them as symbols on your hands and bind them on your foreheads

❤ You can buy lots of T-shirts, hats and jewelry with Christian messages. My children chose not to wear the T-shirt for the anti-drug program at school. Instead they wore shirts with Bible verses expressing *why* they didn't use drugs.

❤ We encouraged our children not to wear worldly attire, such as T-shirts with computer game heroes or popular name brands. First impressions stick in people's minds and they should reflect Christ in their appearance.

❤ Teach your children to dress in such a way that it doesn't attract attention to themselves. Because of the society we live in, there are a lot of idols. We encouraged our boys not to wear specific sports team symbols or emblems so that their minds were not focused on things of this world (Colossians 3:2).

Write them on the doorframes of your houses and on your gates

♥ I have never covered my walls with cardboard memory verses, like my grandmother. I do, however, hang paintings with Scripture or reminders of the Lord in our home. One example that hung in our kitchen for years is a small plaque with the words "Christ is the unseen guest at our table and the unseen listener of every word." A boy who lived with us for many years called after he had been away for a while and asked, "Is Christ still the unseen guest in your house?" I recall always wanting to eat on a plate that had the face of Jesus on it at my great grandmother's house. Items like these can comfort a child and help keep his mind on God.

♥ Do not allow your child to decide on his own what posters and pictures he hangs in his bedroom. I am amazed at what some Christians allow their children to hang in their rooms. The Bible tells us, "The eye is the lamp of the body. If your eyes are good, your whole body will be full of light" (Matthew 6:22). The things our children see continually will fill their minds and hearts.

♥ Younger children enjoy drawing, painting and cutting out pictures. Have your child make his own posters with Scripture verses and illustrations.

Before God gave the commandment to impress His commands on our children, He walked with Abraham as a father walks with a son. He reasoned with him, made promises and tested Abraham. Later, Abraham could do the same with his son Isaac. Imagine Abraham walking along with Isaac. Abraham told his son all of the promises that God had given him and how he would become a great nation. They must have reasoned together often. The Bible tells us that Isaac asked his father questions one day when they went up the mountain:

> Abraham took the wood for the burnt offering and placed it on his son Isaac, and he himself carried the fire and the knife. As the two of them went on together, Isaac spoke up and said to his father Abraham, "Father?"
> "Yes, my son?" Abraham replied.
> "The fire and wood are here," Isaac said, "but where is the lamb for the burnt offering?"
> Abraham answered, "God himself will provide the lamb for the burnt offering, my son." And the two of them went on together. (Genesis 22:6-8)

Isaac, accustomed to questioning his father, could trust Abraham's answers. By the time they reached their destination, Isaac could quietly surrender as his father placed him on the altar. Allowing our children to question, teaching them as we walk along the way, prepares their hearts for the time when they must surrender their lives completely to God.

Our society has changed dramatically. When I attended elementary school, we were still allowed to pray. Today children carry guns and kill each other. Tim and I earnestly sought God's will for our children and felt we needed to send them to the public school arena. We believe that the effort we made to do the things I discuss in this book helped our children overcome the world in and out of school (1 John 5:3-4). In the closing section I will share how practicing the spiritual disciplines can produce a harvest of righteousness in the teenage years.

In the chapters that follow, we will examine each of the parts of our being—heart, mind, soul and strength. I've chosen to discuss three of the spiritual disciplines in each of these areas. Of course, all the disciplines affect the whole person, but I feel that some can have more impact on our minds, while others have more impact on our hearts, and so on.

No doubt as you read the suggestions given in this book God will put more ideas on your heart. Like Martha, there are a lot of things we need to do—it's a lot of hard work to teach kids to love God! But walking along the way with our children in the presence of God makes it all worth it.

The Narrow Path

Scripture reading: 1 Peter 2:2

Spiritual Guides

The feeding of the child is the work of the tenderest love. The child is pressed to the breast and is held in the closest fellowship with the mother. . . . Even so, the very life and power of God is found in His Word. Through the Word, His tender love will receive us into the gentlest and most intimate fellowship with Himself. From the Word, His love will give us what is needed for our weakness. For the disciple who receives the Word and trustfully relies on Jesus to teach him by the Spirit, the Word of God will prove to be as gentle, sweet milk for new born infants. (Andrew Murray, *The Master's Inner Dwelling*)

Light on the Path

But I have stilled and quieted my soul; like a weaned child with its mother, like a weaned child is my soul within me. (Psalm 131:2)

1. How much do you crave the Word of God?
2. Think of a time when the Scriptures have quieted your soul. Do you recall the particular passage? What was it and why did it still your heart?

Your Traveling Companion

Ask God, *What things do I crave more than Your Word?*

Chapter Four

HEART TO HEART

L ong before the invention of ultrasound, the psalmist wrote:

> For you created my inmost being;
>   you knit me together in my mother's womb.
> I praise you because I am fearfully and wonderfully made;
>   your works are wonderful,
>   I know that full well.
> My frame was not hidden from you
>   when I was made in the secret place.
>   (Psalm 139:13-15)

For an unborn child, the womb is a very secure, warm environment. A fetus learns to ignore many noises and sensations. Through ultrasound a mother can watch her child's reaction to outside stimuli. A baby jerks and his heart rate goes up when he hears a loud noise. If the sound continues, he grows accustomed to it. Mothers have reported that their children remembered music that they heard repeatedly before birth. A newborn will instinctively turn his head toward his mother or father's voice, even if there are other adults speaking.

Psalm 139 continues in verse 23, "Search me, O God, and know my heart." Could it be that God searches our hearts, even from the womb? If this is true, then how can parents play a part in this process? Is it possible to recognize some personality traits in a child from the womb? I think so. If God "knits" a child in the womb, he must be weaving his temperament as well as his body. Less than a week before Joshua's birth, my doctor informed me that the baby was breech and I would probably need a C-section. That evening, Tim and I had a little talk with our baby and "together" we all prayed for the Lord's intervention.

Later, as Tim slept peacefully beside me, I watched the baby somersault into the correct position. Yes, his acrobatic performance was painful, but worth it. My amazed doctor could hardly believe what he saw a few days later.

Was God just taking care of our health? I think it was more than that. I believe at that moment God placed a strong will and determination in Joshua's heart. It's as if He knitted a stubborn streak into this child that Joshua has carried throughout his life. Because of this little "miracle" during my pregnancy, Tim and I were not surprised at the things we have had to deal with in Joshua's personality. As he has grown, we have watched the Lord change our son's tenacious spirit into a wholehearted zeal for the gospel.

What kinds of behaviors can we expect to recognize in a child while he grows inside the womb? Psalm 58:3 says, "Even from birth the wicked go astray; from the womb they are wayward and speak lies." To be honest, I don't think I could or would want to recognize such traits in my child. But this Scripture does support the idea that a child's personality develops at a very early stage.

The Bible clearly teaches that a child's heart is sinful from birth (see, for example, Psalm 51:5 and Proverbs 22:15). It's the job of parents to take advantage of a child's innate knowledge of right and wrong (Romans 2:15) and point it toward God. Watching closely a child's personality traits can give clues as to which way his heart tends to bend.

Of course, parents have no way of knowing exactly what personality traits the Lord has planned for their children, but we can certainly ask Him. When Isaac asked the Lord to open his wife's barren womb, God answered in a big way—twins! The Bible says that these babies "jostled each other within her." Rebekah must have felt worn out as she went to "inquire of the LORD" to find out what was happening inside her. The Lord told her that she carried two nations who would fight and compete with each other their entire lives (Genesis 25:21-26).

God warned Rebekah that her younger twin would be stronger. Even at birth he grabbed his brother's heel trying to be first and his mother named him Jacob, meaning "he deceives." If you read the rest of their story, you'll notice that the traits of selfishness and deception stayed with Jacob his entire life—or at least until his life-changing encounter with God at Peniel (32:22-30). From the story of Jacob we can see that personality traits are indeed formed in the womb. What better time to begin practicing the spiritual disciplines in a child's life? Another thing we learn from Jacob is that God is able to temper and sanctify our personality traits, if we let Him. All the more reason to encourage the development of spiritual disciplines at an early age.

All Your Heart

Children understand the concept of *all* at a very young age. They want *all* their toys. They eat *all* their cookies, while refusing to eat *all* their vegetables. God commanded that we love Him with *all* our hearts. Remember that God doesn't want ninety percent of our hearts. He desires 100 percent! Our job as parents is to help our children remove things in their hearts that fill God's place.

I think it is a mistake to teach our children to "put God first." As a child, I recall singing in Sunday school J-O-Y, "Jesus first; Yourself last; and Others in between." Later as an adult, I struggled to keep my priorities straight—God first, family second and so on. God kept conveying to my heart that He didn't want to compete for the top of my list—He wanted to be the *entire* list!

Once I set my list aside and sought to love God with all my heart, He began to direct and bless the other aspects of my life. Throwing away my list of priorities brought a tremendous freedom. This led to a decision not to teach my children to "keep their priorities straight," but rather to give their whole hearts to God and allow Him to direct their lives.

Wouldn't it be nice if we had a "spiritual ultrasound" that could peek into the hearts of our children to see what things might keep them from loving God wholeheartedly? We could see where they were "naughty or nice" and deal with them accordingly. Unfortunately, if such a thing were possible, we might not always like what we see.

As you get to know your child, certain personality traits will emerge. Research has shown that by the age of three the personality of a child is clearly defined. Often those traits are learned from their parents.[1] Have you ever felt that you were looking in a mirror when watching your child? Perhaps the Holy Spirit's revelation of our own behavior is the "ultrasound" that gives insight into our children's hearts.

Fortunately, our children's behavior—as well as our own—can be changed through the power of Jesus Christ. We will talk in a later chapter how the spiritual disciplines can steer a child's heart toward God. But first let's look at a few heart characteristics we might recognize in a child.

The heart muscle pumps life through our physical bodies. We think of it as the center of our bodies. Likewise, the spiritual heart is the core of a person. It's the center where feelings, emotions and motives drive the life. It takes a willingness to see our children's hearts clearly, even if we discover we do not like what we see. By understanding a child's personality traits, we can help him love God with all his heart.

Like Rebekah, we can ask God what He plans to knit in our child as he grows inside the womb. During pregnancy, watch for signs indicating personality traits of your unborn child. Journal your baby's movements and habits during pregnancy. You might be surprised to see some of the same patterns throughout his life. During my pregnancy with Josiah, he kept me awake every night with hiccups and aerobics.

Later as a toddler, it seemed impossible to get my son to bed before 10 o'clock every night.

At the time a young woman separated from her abusive husband found shelter in our home. She returned from work in the evening around the time I was ready for bed. I didn't have the energy to keep her company, but Josiah, getting his second wind, would chatter up a storm while she wound down. I felt like a terrible mother allowing my child to stay up so late, and I wouldn't recommend such a habit to new parents. Yet, looking back at his sleep patterns before birth, I realized God had knit this in Josiah for a purpose. He filled a lonely person's life with joy during late-night hours. We began to call him our little "night watchman" (Isaiah 21:11-12). Surprisingly, after the woman left our home, Josiah began to go to bed earlier.

When identifying your baby's temperament, remember not to worry too much about what is "normal." Realize too that your newborn child's motives for his behavior are based on his immediate needs. For example, he's not crying all night just to make you frustrated; how you respond to his crying, however, will lead him to expect the same response to future crying. By recognizing his behavior patterns from birth, you can help steer his motives toward the Lord as your child grows.

Once you understand some of your child's behavior patterns you can begin to instill godly attributes in his heart. I think the first and most important trait we want to instill in a child's heart is honesty. Remember the passage in Psalm 58:3—"from the womb [the wicked] are wayward and speak lies"? One of the hardest things to face is having a child that lies. Dishonesty begins very young, as a child lies to protect himself or cheats to win a game or better his grades. Parents must ask for holy discernment to see the truth. After our oldest left home, I recalled all the times I sensed that he was not telling the truth but let it slip by. When he reached his teen years, I often felt frustrated, knowing my son had lied but not able to prove it.

Shortly after their brother went away, I overheard our two younger sons making a pact to walk in the truth with us in all things. It hasn't always been easy, but they openly share their hearts with us. I can truly say, "I have no greater joy than to hear that my children are walking in the truth" (3 John 1:4).

Whining and tantrums usually start to occur as a child begins to test his boundaries. All my children threw the usual "terrible twos" tantrums when they didn't get their way or were overly tired. Joshua, however, often threw horrendous tantrums—the kind that embarrass a mother in public. That stubborn streak came out in unacceptable ways. Recognizing that small indications of a quick temper were part of the big picture of Joshua's personality helped us to deal with his heart. Inch by inch and incident by incident, we encouraged and admonished Joshua to turn his frustrations over to the Lord. Letting him know we loved him but that we were in charge helped to steer Joshua's independence into dependence on the Lord.

Along with personality traits, take note of your child's likes and dislikes. What kinds of games and toys does he prefer? We were often teased and ridiculed for allowing preschooler Josiah to play with dolls. But as he grew, we saw that the Lord was putting a love for younger children in his heart. At the age of nine he began teaching Sunday school lessons to the younger kids at church. He soon became the "pied piper" with small children following him everywhere.

These are just a few ideas on how to identify and watch your child's heart grow. My children's personality traits became clearer as they grew older. For example, I tried to look at Josiah's extreme messiness as a toddler's exploration of his world. He always made pictures or sculptures out of his food, play-dough, mud—anything that he could mold or squish became an art form. Today at seventeen he is well on his way to becoming a professional artist. As your child chooses friends, careers and life goals, you will be able to see how the Lord was guiding and steering him all his life.

Proverbs 22:15 tells parents, "Folly is bound up in the heart of a child, but the rod of discipline will drive it far from him." We mistakenly think of the term "rod" as solely referring to spanking a child, but a rod can also denote a measurement. As stated before, a child has a part of him that is bent on evil. Foolishness, disobedience and rebellion are bound tight in his heart. Each child needs a certain measure of discipline to loosen up such folly. As Dr. William Sears in his book *Parenting and Child Care* puts it,

> God, our Father, has directed parents to do two things for their children: to teach and to discipline. *Teaching* means to impart God's Word to your children. *Disciplining* goes one step further—it imparts God's Word to your children to such a degree that His Word becomes part of each child's inner self, his inner controls, his base of operations. In short, to discipline a child means to instill a sense of direction.[2]

The spiritual disciplines are the rod that can help parents make God's Word part of their child's heart. Let's look at how the spiritual disciplines of prayer, worship and confession can help our children yield their hearts to God.

Prayer

Though prayer is a learned process we should never make it too complicated. The heart of a child readily accepts that communication with God is a simple process. Richard Foster notes that a childlike heart is an essential element of prayer:

> Jesus taught us to come like children to a father. Openness, honesty, and trust mark the communication of children with their father. The reason God answers prayers is because his children ask. Further, there is an intimacy between parents and children that has room for both seriousness and laughter.[3]

How we communicate with our children will set the example for how they can talk to God. Just as a good father spends daily time with his children, God longs to spend time with us every day. Here are some ways to guide our children into an intimate prayer time with God.

Before Birth

♥ During pregnancy, pray for your child's heart to be receptive to the traits the Lord knits into him.

♥ Pick a time during the day to pray with your unborn infant so that after he is born you have established this habit.

♥ Start putting together a *Quiet Time Box* before your child is born. (See Appendix C.) Put items for the box on your gift list for your baby.

♥ If you haven't already, begin to cultivate contemplative prayer in your own life. Once your child arrives, along with midnight feedings, diaper changes, ear infections and the like, it will be much harder to fulfill Psalm 62:5—"Find rest, O my soul, in God alone; my hope comes from him."

Infancy to Preschool: Newborn to Age 5

♥ If you didn't establish a time of daily prayer with your child during your pregnancy, do so now. I cannot stress this enough. It may seem ritualistic at first, but daily prayer will soon become a natural part of your child's life. On one of my particularly "down" days after our oldest son left home, God impressed on my heart that my son heard His voice every morning because I had taught him the truth of Isaiah 50:4: "He wakens me morning by morning, wakens my ear to listen like one being taught." It gave me hope to think the habits I had instilled in my son might help draw him back to God.

♥ As your child begins to sit up on his own, introduce the *Quiet Time Box*. I will describe this in detail in the chapter on loving God with all our minds. During this daily routine, the habit of prayer besides nighttime and meals is implanted in a child's heart.

❤ Pray spontaneously when the occasion arises. Let your children see you stop to thank God for His blessings and intervention. (My kids insist that I'm going to cause a major accident some day, breaking out in prayer while driving!)

❤ Whenever your child does something praiseworthy, raise your hands and say, "Praise the Lord!"

❤ Make a picture prayer list of people and things your child wants to pray about and use it during devotional time.

❤ Remember that you want to establish a habit of prayer that leads to a desire to pray to God, not a rule.

Early Childhood: Ages 6-8

❤ If your child has established a daily Quiet Time at this point, he may be ready to graduate from the Quiet Time Box to a more independent devotional time.

❤ Make a point to occasionally plan your private prayer time when your children can see you praying so they can learn from your example.

❤ Pray with your child about things that concern him. Friends and activities at school usually occupy a child's mind at this age.

❤ Teach your child to pray intercessory prayers for people outside his immediate circle. We made a prayer journal with pictures of missionaries and of the child we supported through an international Christian relief agency.

❤ Allow your child to pick his own "prayer closet"—a place where he can talk to God without distraction.

❤ Children at this age may want to start having their Quiet Time without you. One day I awoke to find six-year-old Joshua missing from his bed. Concerned, I searched the quiet, dark house and found my son kneeling in the living room, praying. When Joshua noticed me, he ran over and gave me a big hug. With a smile as bright as the sun dawning in the window he said, "Good morning, Mom! I set my alarm for 6 o'clock so I could get a quiet time alone with God."

Middle Years: Ages 9-12

❤ Gradually release your child to have a daily quiet time by himself. Although I was pleased that Joshua got up early on his own to pray, I still had quiet times with him several days a week until I felt he was ready for total independence.

❤ Don't be surprised if at this age your child tends to balk at having daily devotions. Every one of my kids did. As they took more responsibility for their own schedules, homework and belongings, their daily routines became full. I tried not to let them go longer than two days without private prayer time. Usually a gentle reminder or a devotional with Mom or Dad got my kids back to their regular quiet time routine.

❤ Allow your child freedom in deciding how he wants to spend time alone with God. I offered my children different options for their quiet times, such as blank books for journaling, writing letters to God, drawing pictures of things they were thankful for, and age-appropriate devotionals.

❤ Teach your child to keep track of their prayers and how God answers them.

❤ Prayer becomes more personal at this stage. Make suggestions on things your child can pray about, such as a spelling test or friends at school.

❤ Read The Lord's Prayer (Matthew 6:9-13). Have your child rewrite this prayer in his own words.

💜 Introduce contemplative prayer by encouraging your child to have times of silence before God. Bedtime is a great time to start this practice. We didn't allow our children to have a lot of toys or listen to music at bedtime, but instead encouraged them to think of how the Lord had blessed their day. "On my bed I remember you; I think of you through the watches of the night" (Psalm 63:6).

💜 Ask your children to help you write a list of needs or concerns. Then, like Hezekiah, "spread it out before the LORD" (2 Kings 19:14). Focus your prayer time on thanking God for working in these situations, rather than listing them out loud in prayer.

💜 It's really easy for dinner prayers to become ritualistic. In our family we say a prayer prior to the meal, then we read a Bible verse. After the meal, no one is allowed to be dismissed from the table until Dad gives permission, which allows for good fellowship as a family. When the meal is over, we either pray as a family or each of us prays silently before leaving. This is in accordance with Deuteronomy 8:10: "When you have eaten and are satisfied, praise the LORD your God for the good land he has given you." It's easy to pray when you are hungry, but this helps us to remember God when our stomachs are full.

Worship

The purpose of worship is to give back to God a small portion of what He has given to us. It is our response to His love. God longs for us to worship Him. "Yet a time is coming and has now come when the true worshipers will worship the Father in spirit and truth, for they are the kind of worshipers the Father seeks" (John 4:23).

Worship reaches beyond the formal weekly service. It reaches every corner of our lives and leads us into the presence of God. Brother Lawrence knew the importance of worshiping God in everything he did.

We should be considerate of God in everything we do and say. Our goal should be to become perfect in our adoration of Him throughout this earthly life in preparation for all eternity.[4]

Setting the example of thanksgiving and worship toward God helps your child focus his heart on Him. Here are some ways to guide your child to worship God throughout his day:

Before Birth

💜 Take advantage of this time in life to understand the depth of God's awesomeness. When your body aches or you feel blue, spend time in worship and adoration toward God for the gift of life. "A cheerful heart is good medicine, but a crushed spirit dries up the bones" (Proverbs 17:22).

💜 Sing songs of praise. Your child will remember your voice after he is born; some parents believe that children can even recall the songs they sang during pregnancy.

💜 Meditate on the first commandment to love the Lord your God with all your heart, soul, mind and strength so that you have a proper perspective worshiping God.

Infancy to Preschool: Newborn to Age 5

💜 The *Quiet Time Box* devotional time introduces a very young child to worship. Sing songs and raise your hands in praise to the Lord.

💜 At this age we teach our children to say "please" and "thank you." Remind them to say "thank you" to the Lord throughout their day. For instance, when they accomplish a task or hear a bird sing you can encourage them to worship and thank God. Instilling thankfulness in a child's heart for God's blessings sets him on the path of loving Him with all his heart.

❤ Of course, talk to your baby as you go through your daily routine. ("Let's change your diaper." "Are you hungry?") But also add phrases like, "This is the day the Lord has made, let's rejoice and be glad," or "Jesus loves you." Your child will begin to associate not only words with his environment, but the Lord's name with comfort and trust.

❤ Make a "Thank You, God" poster by pasting pictures of people and things your child is thankful for and hang it where it can be easily seen.

Early Childhood: Ages 6-8

❤ At this stage a child will begin to separate his parents from God. He starts to understand that God is his personal Creator and Savior and deserves to be worshiped.

❤ Include your child in congregational, personal and family worship experiences.

❤ Guide your child in preparing for worship. On the night before you attend worship services, have your child lay out his special clothing, Bible and Sunday school papers. This makes worship a special occasion.

❤ Read the story of Solomon rebuilding the temple and gathering the people to worship there (1 Kings 8). Emphasize how the people were "glad in heart" (8:66) from worshiping the Lord.

❤ Teach your child words like *merciful, loving, forgiving* and *kind* to describe God. In our house the word "awesome" is reserved for God and not for something man does.

Middle Years: Ages 9-12

❤ During this age, children enjoy participating in worship services. By now you recognize and appreciate your child's personality strengths. Find ways that your child can participate and feel part of the worship experience. Our son Josiah, for example, helped out with Sunday school as a pre-teen.

♥   Your child's friends at school may talk about their beliefs. He might start to compare your forms of worship with those of others. Allow your child to question and explore his own way of worshiping God, under your close guidance.

♥   Continue to model worship outside of the formal setting. My children know I can start to pray or sing as I'm driving down the road. (My teenagers joke that they enjoyed hearing my singing when they were little, but now it hurts their ears!)

♥   If your child is having independent devotional times at this stage, ask to join him occasionally. But don't worry if your child guards this time. My friend Jeanne said that her daughter became adamant about having time alone with God. At first she worried about what Christine might be doing or confessing to God. But as she saw her daughter's spiritual growth, she realized that Christine was worshiping and communing with God during her quiet times.

Confession

Confession is probably the most difficult of the spiritual disciplines. We fight against revealing our failures and sins to others. When we struggle with temptation, we believe that we are the only ones who are so terrible. We often say that we belong to a fellowship of believers, but first we belong to a fellowship of sinners. Romans 3:23 tells us, "for all have sinned and fall short of the glory of God." It is in the body of Christ that we find healing. "Therefore confess your sins to each other and pray for each other so that you may be healed. The prayer of a righteous man is powerful and effective" (James 5:16).

Often people will say, "Confession is between me and God." This is true; Christ is our Mediator. But God has made a special way for us to feel His forgiveness. In our house we call it "walking in the light."

If we claim to have fellowship with him yet walk in the dark-
ness, we lie and do not live by the truth. But if we walk in the
light, as he is in the light, we have fellowship with one another, and the blood of Jesus, his Son, purifies us from all sin.

If we claim to be without sin, we deceive ourselves and the
truth is not in us. If we confess our sins, he is faithful and just
and will forgive us our sins and purify us from all unrighteousness. (1 John 1:6-9)

Through confession, we feel forgiveness and purification. Joshua
struggles and wrestles with the normal teenage temptations. One day
he said that he could see how his older brother deceived us. He confessed that, at times, deception was a temptation for him, too.
Ironically, Joshua's confession was a way of resisting the very temptation he was admitting to. By "walking in the light," making our lives an
open book before God and others, temptation loses much of its power.

Before Birth

♥ Pray Psalm 139:23-24: *Search me, O God, and know my heart;
  test me and know my anxious thoughts. See if there is any
  offensive way in me, and lead me in the way everlasting.*
  Pregnancy can be an anxious time. Use this time to find
  cleansing in your own heart toward God.

♥ Promise God that you will teach your child to "walk in the light"
  and will not fear seeing things that might be hard to accept.

Infancy to Preschool: Newborn to Age 5

♥ At this stage, confession begins by teaching a child the
  difference between acceptable and unacceptable behavior.
  "No!" often becomes the first word a child will say because it's
  the first word he hears the most. He quickly learns what
  behaviors get him the most attention. Try to alternate "No" with
  phrases like "Stop," "Give that to Mama, please," or "Let's play

with something else." Praise him for being good so that he learns the response he gets for acceptable behavior.

❤ Once a child understands the consequences of unacceptable behavior, you can teach him to say, "I'm sorry." When Joshua was around two years old, he hurt our dog. Tim told him to say he was sorry to the pup and showed him how to gently pet it. Joshua puckered his lips and crossed his arms and refused to apologize. It then became a power struggle, with his father's authority at stake. Tim stood firm and began showing affection to the dog. Joshua then realized that his relationship had been broken not only between himself and his pet, but with his father as well, and he apologized.

❤ Teach your child about forgiveness. God has given us the authority to forgive one another. "If you forgive anyone his sins, they are forgiven; if you do not forgive them, they are not forgiven" (John 20:23). Your child will learn God's forgiveness by feeling forgiveness from you.

Early Childhood: Ages 6-8

❤ Take the time to explain the "why" of your rules. This concept really starts much earlier, but at this age children begin to reason back with their parents.

❤ Save disciplines, reprimands and confessions for significant incidents and truly sinful behavior. Breaking your favorite dish has no eternal consequences; lying about it does.

❤ Teach your child to value "godly sorrow" over "worldly sorrow" (2 Corinthians 7:10-11). Children sometimes admit their mistakes only because they hope to avoid punishment. Have you ever heard a child scream, "I'm sorry, I'm sorry," knowing full well he's only sorry he got caught? Teach him that godly sorrow leads to repentance and changed behavior.

Middle Years: Ages 9-12

💜 Expect and encourage your child to "walk in the light" in small things, such as bad attitudes, envying other kids or stretching the truth. Don't wait until the little things have added up to a big problem. "Little white lies" usually become long strings of deceit.

💜 On the other hand, don't think you have to deal with every situation as it occurs. Sometimes it is more effective to wait until a similar incident happens. We discovered that waiting for God to tug at our children's hearts often brings a deeper confession and more lasting repentance than immediately confronting each instance of misbehavior. This is especially true with things that can plague a child's conscience, such as lying or hurting someone.

💜 Often as parents we sense that our child is hiding something from us. Don't be afraid to wait on the Lord to bring the details to light instead of forcing him to confess.

💜 At this age you can begin to confess the "sins of your youth" with your child, depending on his sensitivity and vulnerability to such things. Be careful not to glorify your sins in front of your child, but model a heart of transparency and repentance.

💜 Teach your child that he can go to God in private confession. Read his journals only by invitation. Encourage him to come to you with nagging thoughts or habits of sin.

💜 Emphasize to your child that because all of us "have sinned and fall short of the glory of God" (Romans 3:23), there is nothing he could say or do that you or God would not forgive him for.

Tim and I have always told our children that they must love God with all their hearts. God is love and the source of all love (1 John 4:16). Any love we have for each other outside of that true source of love is fleshly and carnal. When we fill our hearts with God's love then our love for each other becomes pure and unselfish. Through the disciplines of prayer, worship and confession we can teach our children to focus on God. He wants to fill their hearts so that there is room for nothing else. Our hope is that they will say with the Psalmist, "Create in me a pure heart, O God, and renew a steadfast spirit within me" (Psalm 51:10).

The Narrow Path

Scripture reading: Psalm 19:14

Spiritual Guides

> We might say that "the heart" is the real person. It is "pure" when all the pretense, masks, regulated behaviors, old concepts and guards, are stripped away. (Peter Lord, *Hearing God*)

Light on the Path

> The LORD your God will circumcise your hearts and the hearts of your descendants, so that you may love him with all your heart and with all your soul, and live. (Deuteronomy 30:6)

1. Ask God to show you the areas in your heart that need circumcising.
2. How can prayer, worship and confession lead you to have a pure heart?
3. How much of your prayer time is spent in speaking rather than listening to God? Experiment with listening to God more.

Your Traveling Companion

Pray with Richard Foster:

Loving Lord, as I begin this journey into a prayer-filled life, please be with me—guarding and guiding. Protect me, O God, from all evil. Surround me with the light of Christ, cover me with the blood of Christ, seal me with the cross of Christ. This I ask in the name of Christ. Amen.[5]

Chapter Five

A DISCIPLINED MIND

One day as I watched my ten-month-old son playing on the floor, I realized that Joshua might struggle with learning disabilities. Since I had worked with disabled children for many years, I recognized some of the signs. For instance, Joshua found it difficult to exchange toys from one hand to the other or to pick up small objects. As he entered school, I requested that he be tested, but the teachers kept reassuring me that *all* children reverse letters and numbers at this age. Finally, at the end of second grade, Joshua's teacher agreed that we needed to dig for answers to his difficulties.

The tests revealed that Joshua had some serious processing problems that would cause him to struggle with learning all his life. Tim and I had never placed an emphasis on good grades. We just wanted our children to do the best they could. But now we realized our son might not even learn to read well or write clearly. Since we knew that God had formed our child in the womb and was sovereign over his life, we resolved to find out God's plan for Joshua.

Like all parents, I wanted to believe that my child was healthy and intelligent. As I began to accept that my son might not win a Nobel Prize, I asked myself, *What kind of wisdom do I really want my children to have, anyway?* I began to search the Scriptures about wisdom

that comes from God and realized the type of wisdom I should desire
my children to acquire.

> For the message of the cross is foolishness to those who
> are perishing, but to us who are being saved it is the power of
> God. For it is written:
>
> "I will destroy the wisdom of the wise;
>   the intelligence of the intelligent I will frustrate."
>
> Where is the wise man? Where is the scholar? Where is
> the philosopher of this age? Has not God made foolish the
> wisdom of the world? For since in the wisdom of God the
> world through its wisdom did not know him, God was
> pleased through the foolishness of what was preached to
> save those who believe. (1 Corinthians 1:18-21)

It didn't take long for Tim and me to see that, just as Paul's "thorn in
the flesh" kept him humble (2 Corinthians 12:7), God had knitted
learning disabilities in Joshua in order to keep him dependent on God's
wisdom. His stubbornness and independent spirit needed a bridle to
keep him in control. Having to struggle through school was God's gift
to our son. He learned quickly not to worry about what others thought
of him. His intelligence was frustrated and he cried out to God for help.

Remember the old slogan, "A mind is a terrible thing to waste"? Jesus illustrated the truth of this when He added the element *mind* to the
commandment to love the Lord with all your heart, soul and strength.
A child's mind will get filled, that's for certain. It's our job as parents
to decide just what will take up the space in our children's little heads.
We may not always be able to change a child's heart, but filling his
mind with God's Word gives us a running start.

Filling your child's mind with the things of the Lord can begin as
early as birth. What a wonderful stage in life! During infancy you can
expect to see responses from your child to the many things you strive to
teach him. Sometime around six to nine months a child can start to sit

with little or no support. During this time, he begins to work on mastering mobility. Once he discovers he can move around—watch out! Life will never be the same. You can take advantage of this learning time to fill his little mind with spiritual truths and lessons.

A baby learns very early the process of *habituation*—the repetition of particular stimuli or experiences. His memory lengthens and he associates behavior with consequences. For example, he knows you will respond when he cries. You know this to be true by the late-night hours you keep, right? We will look at ways parents can begin to instill the habits of prayer, meditation and Bible study beginning as young as six months. Such habits fill a young child's mind with a love for God.

In a later chapter we will discuss how a child's intellectual strengths can turn him toward God. But for now, let's concentrate on the things that tend to fill our children's minds. Let's start with the obvious—television.

Most Christians, and even a lot of non-Christians, would agree that television is not the best thing for our kids. But how many of us really pay attention to what fills our kids' minds through television? I am not saying we should all smash the "one-eyed monster"—although, for some families, it might not be a bad idea. Instead, we need to seriously evaluate what fills our children's minds while watching television. Ecclesiastes 7:18 tells us, "The man who fears God will avoid all extremes."

I mentioned before that Joshua had quite the temper when he was younger. One day I happened to walk by as he watched *Sesame Street*. On the screen a goat was jumping up and down saying, "I'm mad! I'm mad! It's OK to be mad!" (I understand, of course, that the intent of the cartoon was to teach that anger is a normal emotion. But such a complex concept would go over preschoolers' heads. They see the goat jumping up and down, and get the message that it's OK to throw a temper tantrum!)

Click! Off went the television. Joshua was about three and a half at the time and I admit I felt like I had fired my baby-sitter that day. But it made me realize how subtly television teaches our kids values we don't want them to have.

Tim and I have had the advantage of scrutinizing our children's television viewing all their lives. It's very challenging for parents who become Christians when their children are preteens or teens to try to control their entertainment choices. In his book, *Worldly Amusements*, pastor and television production expert, Wayne A. Wilson, encourages such parents.

> For some children who have been immersed in the world it may take long years of sad experience to finally reject the world. It is a battle, but it must be waged. Set the example. Learn to communicate the value of a pure mind and heart. . . . Respond with sincerity and humor. Be big-hearted, not rigid and narrow. But don't compromise.[1]

We have some friends who made a decision to clean up their television viewing. Their three children's ages range from nine to seventeen. Before setting down rules for their kids about their entertainment, the parents felt the Lord's leading to fast from all television for two weeks. After that time their children would also fast from this media. They had already planned a vacation prior to starting the fast. This family returned from their break refreshed, because it was the first time they had not spent the entire time "glued to the TV." They hiked, read books and the Bible, and communicated with one another. They all agreed it was the best vacation they had ever had.

While television definitely has its downside, it can also be a wonderful tool for teaching children. Our video library includes Bible stories and Scripture tapes. Striving to follow the warning from Ecclesiastes to avoid all extremes, we didn't take away television completely, but monitored what our children watched.

In order to avoid extremes we sought God's guidance on how to apply the rod of discipline. Remember that "folly is bound up in the heart of a child, but the rod of discipline will drive it far from him" (Proverbs

22:15). As mentioned in the last chapter, a rod can represent punishment and discipline, but it was also a tool for measurement. It cannot be repeated enough that it takes a certain measure or amount of discipline to drive the folly far from the heart of a child. Children are naturally attracted to things that will fill their minds with folly—such as video games, television, comic books—the list is endless.

Each child is different. One child might be more prone to violence while another might be very gentle. One four-year-old boy who spent time in our home seemed to always like the dark side of things. For example, one day as I read a storybook about David and Goliath he became totally entranced with the picture of David cutting off the giant's head. "Boy, look at that knife! I bet that would make a lot of blood!" (There was no blood in the picture.) Even the other children were amazed at the boy's response. So the measurement or rod of discipline for him was to screen TV, video games and books carefully so that his mind might begin to focus on God and not violence.

It takes a lot of humility to know the right amount of discipline that will help a child's mind and heart focus on God. None of us have all the answers and we all make mistakes. But we have the promise that God will give us wisdom when we ask (James 1:5). And I believe that there is no role in life that needs God's wisdom more than parenting.

Asking God for wisdom is definitely a way for parents to practice praying continually (1 Thessalonians 5:17). My constant prayer as I lead my children is *Lord, please give me wisdom.* God has generously answered that prayer by showing my husband and me how to teach our children to practice the disciplines of meditation, study and solitude.

Meditation

In the Bible meditation is simply drawing close to God and His Word. The spiritual discipline of meditation quiets our souls to hear God's voice. Many believers, however, shy away from meditation because of its association with Eastern religions and New Age practices.

Satan is the deceiver. If he cannot convince us to follow a lie, he will produce a parody of the truth to scare us away from the real thing. Most

Christians sense that Eastern meditation practices, which emphasize losing yourself in order to "become one with the Cosmic Mind," reek of sulfur and brimstone. But as a result, we tend to steer clear of meditation altogether. One reason for this hesitation is because meditation depends on the imagination. Jan Johnson, a spiritual director and retreat speaker, says,

> Some Christians object to meditation because it uses the imagination. It is wiser, however, to give our imagination to God to be retrained by Him than to withhold it. The process of spiritual formation allows every part of our being to be embraced and schooled by God, and the imagination needs retraining as much as anything else. If we ignore our imagination, it finds entertainment of its own. When activated by the images and truths of Scripture, the imagination enables the penetrating Word of God to become active in our lives.[2]

Children have wonderful imaginations. While they are still young, we have the opportunity to train their imaginations to focus on the Lord. When Josiah turned two I decided it was time for him to give up the pacifier. For several nights, he cried for the old friend before going to bed, and I would encourage him to think of Christ. "Trust in Jesus," I told him. Finally one night Josiah told me, "Twust in Jesus" and I thought we had won.

At the time we had a home fellowship meeting in our house. Sunday rolled around with lots of pacifiers in the mouths of other babies. Naturally Josiah wanted his own back. As our worship services began, Josiah began to really fuss. He wanted his pacifier, but asked to get his book on faith and his blanket, which he never carried. So I gave him permission to run up to his room for his treasures so he would settle down.

Soon we could hear Josiah screaming from upstairs. I sent his big brother to check out the situation. When they returned, my oldest son whispered to me, "He says he saw Jesus."

He said what? I thought. *Oh, well, at least he is content.* I continued worshiping. After church we asked our toddler what had happened. He very casually replied, "I saw Jesus" and ran upstairs to show us. Josiah pointed to a window and said, "There! He was holding a baby. That baby me!" Josiah never asked for his pacifier again.

Now whether God blessed our young son with an actual vision or not doesn't really matter. Teaching him to meditate on Jesus in his time of need helped him to use his imagination to focus on Christ's love and comfort. Try these ideas for sanctifying the imagination in order to teach your child to love God with all his mind.

Before Birth

♥ Use this time to "retrain" your own imagination. Realize that the imagination can be untrustworthy at times and can be used by Satan to deceive. Bring your imagination under the control of the Holy Spirit so that you will be prepared to steer your child's imagination later.

♥ When you are pregnant, everyone seems to have "horror" stories about their own pregnancy. I started working with developmentally disabled children when I was fifteen and had my first child at nineteen. During that pregnancy, I battled with fears of the "what ifs." I adored the kids at the clinic, but what if my own child had a handicap? I recalled seeing the struggles that parents of my special kids faced, and I wasn't sure I could handle it. By the time my other two children came along, I knew how to meditate on the Word of God to deal with such fears.

♥ Meditate on the parables of Jesus and think of the images He used to convey His message. I recall imagining myself holding my children before they were born, natural thoughts for an expectant mother. Ask God to show you now how to lead your little one to Him. Imagine yourself reading the Bible or singing songs of praise to your newborn child.

Infancy to Preschool: Newborn to Age 5

❤ Save some of the wonderful children's books on the market for during the day. Read stories from the Bible, however, to your child at bedtime so that he meditates on God's provision and love as he drifts off to sleep.

❤ Babies are born to learn. From the moment your child enters the world he begins exploring through all of his senses. Your baby learns about his surroundings through seeing, hearing, feeling, smelling and tasting. Play games with your child to enhance his senses and learn to use them in meditation. A.W. Tozer wrote:

> The same terms are used to express the knowledge of God as are used to express knowledge of physical things. "O *taste* and *see* that the LORD is good" (Psalm 34:8, emphasis added). "All thy garments *smell* of myrrh, and aloes, and cassia, out of the ivory palaces" (45:8). "My sheep *hear* my voice" (John 10:27, emphasis added). "Blessed are the pure in heart, for they shall *see* God" (Matthew 5:8, emphasis added).[3]

❤ Take walks with your child, allowing him to explore at his own pace. Talk to him about how God made the sky, grass and trees. These memories and words will later tumble around in his thoughts and dreams.

Early Childhood: Ages 6-8

❤ Start each day by reminding your child that "This is the day that the Lord has made," so that he focuses his thoughts on the Lord.

❤ Hang pictures of Bible characters and events in your child's room. It can have the most surprising effects. A friend of mine who works with disabled children says that whenever she shows a picture of Jesus to a particular severely handicapped boy, he breaks out in a big smile.

❤ Start forming a habit of having your child spend time with God every morning and also after school. During summer months, we often stopped our activities in the middle of the day for a time of prayer or Bible reading.

❤ Have your children dress up as their favorite Bible character and meditate on how that person might have felt. For example, what might have been the sights and sounds surrounding David as he walked out to meet Goliath?

Middle Years: Ages 9-12

❤ Determine that you will emphasize your children's spiritual growth over their intellectual growth. Aletha Hinthorn, publisher and founder of *Women Alive Ministries*, notes, "Most Americans value becoming strong intellectually or physically but don't seek to become strong in spirit. Yet Jesus became 'strong in spirit' (Luke 2:40, KJV), and in this world we are to be like Him."[4]

❤ Allow your kids to think for themselves. Don't give the answers right away. Ask questions to help them reason out solutions. This helps them train their imaginations and discipline their minds, enabling them to meditate on God.

❤ Teach your children to "take captive every thought to make it obedient to Christ" (2 Corinthians 10:5). As they become teens, thoughts of insecurities, fears, selfish ambitions and more will creep into their minds. Now is the time to help them learn to control their thoughts, before their thoughts control them.

❤ Tape a Scripture verse on the bathroom mirror or beside your child's morning cereal bowl. My husband started doing this for our children while they were in grade school. By the time they were teens he was leaving them full page letters with passages to meditate on during the day.

I want to make it clear that we taught our children to distinguish between meditation on God and Eastern practices. The boys have been
asked at school, on more than one occasion, to participate in Eastern
meditation. One example took place when Joshua was in the fifth
grade. His music teacher instructed the class to lie down and meditate
and practice relaxation techniques. Our son refused and stood against
the wall. This continued for several days. Each day, however, more
students who professed Christianity joined him at the wall. Soon the
teacher gave up trying to persuade the class to meditate—without any
parental intervention! This incident later opened the door for another
member of the school staff and me to share the gospel with the music
teacher.

Study

The spiritual discipline of study may sometimes intertwine with
meditation, but serves a totally different purpose in helping us to focus
our minds on Christ. When we teach children to meditate, we guide
and encourage them to linger on a passage or thought or experience in
the Lord. When we show them how to study we teach them to interpret
and expound and apply God's Word in their lives. Study gives them the
thoughts and subjects for meditation.

Children learn by repetition. What parent hasn't spent hours with
their child repeating words such as "Mama," "Da Da," "please" and
"thank you"? As a child growing up in the church, I was expected to
memorize and recite the names of the books and select passages of the
Bible. Even to this day, I find myself able to identify the page numbers
of favorite hymns from a hymnal I haven't used in years. Without even
realizing it, repetition affects our inner mind and thought patterns.

Although repeating information over and over, especially for a
child, can train our minds and change behavior, study goes beyond
"head knowledge" or just accumulating a lot of information. It is a
knowledge that leads to discernment and insight into God's Word and
will. It transforms our minds so we can worship and love God. As
Romans 12:1-2 states:

Therefore, I urge you, brothers, in view of God's mercy, to offer your bodies as living sacrifices, holy and pleasing to God—this is your spiritual act of worship. Do not conform any longer to the pattern of this world, but be transformed by the renewing of your mind. Then you will be able to test and approve what God's will is—his good, pleasing and perfect will.

The discipline of study for children includes learning Bible stories and Scriptures, listening to the instruction of their parents and teachers, and reading (or watching) carefully selected material. Practicing this discipline fills children's hearts and minds with the desire to follow God's perfect will in their lives.

Before Birth

❤ If you haven't practiced the discipline of study, begin to do so now. Ask God to give you understanding as you read His Word.

❤ Study books about the growth process of a child so that you might reflect and understand how you can lead your child to God at different stages.

❤ Select and read other books on the spiritual disciplines, such as those listed in Appendix A.

Infancy to Preschool: Newborn to Age 5

❤ Establish a daily quiet time. This will instill strong spiritual habits along with the others your child is learning, such as eating and sleeping at certain times. Why not make prayer and reading God's Word as important to life as food and rest? (See Appendix C.)

❤ Play games for the purpose of not only strengthening your child's skills, but teaching him about God. (See Appendix B.)

❤ Around the age of four your child can begin to graduate from the *Quiet Time Box* to more traditional devotions. I wrote *The Children's Discovery Bible Devotions* (Chariot Victor Books) for children at this stage. (See Appendix A for a list of age-appropriate devotional books.)

❤ Check the teacher resource section in your local Christian bookstore to find age-appropriate activity books that will teach your child simple Bible lessons.

Early Childhood: Ages 6-8

❤ I mentioned earlier the idea of having children dress up as Bible characters. This is a great way to teach kids to study. We kept a box of costumes and props ready for instant fun. The toddlers to the teens loved digging into the Scriptures, Bible handbooks and other materials to make sure their plays were authentic. From this idea I wrote the book *My Bible Dress-up Book* (Cook Communications), which provides stories, trivia and ideas for making costumes for favorite Bible stories.

❤ As a child begins to read, you can gradually wean him from quiet times with you to independent times of praying and reading alone with God. There are many children's Bibles and books on the market that a child can read independently. (See Appendix A for a few suggestions.)

❤ Realize that each child learns in different ways. Observe how your children learn best and find ways to encourage Bible study that fits each individual's learning style. For instance, Joshua's learning disabilities cause him to be a very auditory learner; reading was difficult for him. So I provided Scripture tapes and music for him to learn Bible verses and stories. On the other hand, Josiah has a more random learning style and gathers information in many different ways. I guided his learning through books, pencils and drawing activities.

❤   Make a point to become your child's teacher. Our meal times
     and drives in the car provide some of the best teaching moments
     for understanding Scripture and dealing with life's experiences
     according to God's standards.

❤   Write your own devotions based on your child's individual
     needs. When my kids' folly started coming out in lying, arguing
     or whining, I didn't have time to chase down devotions for a
     particular problem. So I wrote them myself and included
     Scripture, Bible stories and activities relating to my child's
     particular situation.

Solitude

My mother used to tell me that "children are better seen and not
heard." I vowed never to say this to my children, but rather to teach
them the biblical truth taught by the writer of Ecclesiastes that there is
"a time to be silent and a time to speak" (Ecclesiastes 3:7). Teaching
children self-control is the key to solitude. The purpose of silence and
solitude is to enter the rest of God, not to shut ourselves off from the
world. Teaching our children to quiet their hearts and minds helps
them to feel God's presence throughout the day. According to Richard
Foster,

> Solitude is more a state of mind and heart than it is a place.
> There is a solitude of the heart that can be maintained at all
> times. Crowds, or the lack of them, have little to do with this
> inward attentiveness. . . . In the midst of noise and confusion
> we are settled into a deep inner silence. Whether alone or
> among people, we always carry with us a portable sanctuary
> of the heart.[5]

Silence and solitude do not come easily to most of us, even among
those for whom it is a way of life. A hearing-impaired couple we know
used to fill their silence with books, magazines and closed-caption

television. They live in a world of silence, yet were anything but quiet. Their hearing preschooler followed their example and constantly desired to be entertained. They are now learning how to "be still" and discovering the joy of truly knowing God (Psalm 46:10).

If solitude is difficult for adults, it's doubly hard for preschoolers. They may not be able to sit and do nothing, but they can certainly be taught to play quietly alone—besides the "time out corner." I replaced the *Sesame Street* hour with books and tapes that encouraged my boys to think about God. One day shortly after I had clicked off PBS, Joshua was listening to a music tape with a set of large headphones on his ears. I noticed huge tears quietly falling down his cheeks.

When I asked him what was wrong, he said, "Mommy, I'm like Peter! I am stubborn and I have a bad temper. But I want to love Jesus. I really do!" The song told the story of Jesus asking Peter if he loved Him. Peter says he does, but confesses his pride, anger and stubbornness. The goat on television told my son that it was "OK to be mad," but in solitude a Bible story taught my son that he could be freed from his anger and frustration.

Jan Johnson describes solitude like this:

> Silence and solitude both work in hidden ways, resembling the work that goes on during winter. In the cold months, it appears nothing is going on. Animals hibernate. Nothing grows. Everything is still and at rest. But in the important sleep of winter, life renews itself. In silence and solitude, God works in ways that are hidden, but nevertheless vital to life.[6]

I've learned this to be true in my life and my children's lives. Here are some ways that solitude can renew our hearts for the Lord.

Before Birth

♥ Like all spiritual disciplines, solitude is an action, not just a state of mind. Jesus *went* to a "solitary place" (Mark 1:35). He *prayed* on a mountainside "alone" (Matthew 14:23). He *took* his disciples to "a quiet place (to) get some rest" (Mark 6:31). Take this time in your life to learn how to practice solitude, so that you are filled with an inner peace after the birth of your child.

❤ Sometimes it is hard to sleep when you are pregnant. Instead of tossing and turning, think of this as a time of God calling you to be alone with Him.

❤ Find a corner, a chair or a room where you determine that you are going to be silent and in solitude. Or find a place outside your home: a park, beside a lake, the church sanctuary. Return to this spot often. Later, share this place with your child.

❤ During a time of solitude, ask God to help you set goals for your unborn child.

❤ Meditate on James 3:3-13. Ask God to help you control your tongue now, before you even have the chance to become a nagging mother. I know a mother's tongue can sting. I've hurt my own children many times. Practicing silence and solitude helps me to control my speech.

Infancy to Preschool: Newborn to Age 5

❤ Contrary to what a lot of new parents think, it's OK to let a baby cry sometimes. First make certain that all his physical needs are met. Then put him in his crib or playpen for some "alone" time. This is the first step to teaching solitude. After a few times of being alone, his crying will shorten.

❤ Set up a "quiet corner" in your home where your child can play, "read" or listen to tapes. If possible, use this corner for only these times so that your child begins to associate this as time with God. The corner Granny sent me to was an old couch hidden by the dining room table.

❤ Teach your child to be silent on his bed. One night shortly after Josiah's "visit from Jesus," I had difficulty getting him to settle down. "Jesus will help you fall asleep," I encouraged. He quickly retorted with, "I don't see Him!" Holding back a laugh, I said, "Too bad. Faith is being sure of what you don't see so you better just believe." Little ones will sometimes do anything to keep from having to be quiet. Yet teaching them to be still quiets their minds.

Early Childhood: Ages 6-8

♥ A game I like to play at our house or in the car is, "Who Can Be the Quietest?" It works beautifully. And sometimes, I will ask if God spoke to anyone during that time of silence. Some good confession and healing have come out of these mini-retreats.

♥ Teach your children to be quiet as they enter church or times of prayers. "Guard your steps when you go to the house of God. Go near to listen rather than to offer the sacrifice of fools, who do not know that they do wrong" (Ecclesiastes 5:1).

♥ Take your child to a library or bookstore where he is required to sit quietly. This way it can become a special treat to be quiet. Find two chairs and sit quietly with your child reading.

♥ Teach your children contemplative prayer by spending time in silent prayer as a family. Lead them in silence, then ask them to pray one or two word prayers of how they feel about God.

Middle Years: Ages 9-12

♥ Encourage your child to carry the contemplative style of prayer in their private prayer time. One way to do this is to instruct them to pick a favorite Bible verse and focus their thoughts on it.

♥ Reassure your child that he will be distracted as he tries to pray or be silent before the Lord. Share with him your own struggles and what you do when you are distracted. Help him find ways to bring his mind back on the Lord when it wanders. For example, give him a notebook to write down the things that distract him.

As Brother Lawrence wrote, "If your mind wanders at times don't be upset, because being upset will only distract you more. Allow your will to recall your attention gently to God."[7]

❤ At this age, a child may be capable of walking or riding his bike around the neighborhood by himself. Especially after a little spat or a problem, this always helped our kids to focus their minds back in the right direction.

❤ Be cautious to make sure your child is turning toward God and not using solitude as a means of escape from the world or his problems. Have your child make a list of things that make him thankful. Encourage him to think about these things in his solitude. Or have him read a passage of Scripture. The key is withdrawing from the noise and clamor that might distract him from thinking about God.

Brother Lawrence made it his goal to think of nothing but God. He said that if he found his thoughts straying from God, he didn't worry, because he was so unhappy outside of God's presence that he gladly and quickly returned. As our children grow, they will decide whether they desire to give their lives to Christ or not. Filling their minds through meditation, study and solitude with the things that fix their thoughts on Jesus guides their hearts to see that thoughts of anything else are a waste of their minds.

The Narrow Path

Scripture reading: Psalm 26:2-3

Spiritual Guides

[Controlling our mind] is a matter of entering a real battle, so that all our thoughts and ideas are rooted in Jesus and we really attain the stage where we abide in Him. (Basilea Schlink, *You Will Never Be the Same*)

Light on the Path

> We demolish arguments and every pretension that sets itself
> up against the knowledge of God, and we take captive every
> thought to make it obedient to Christ. (2 Corinthians 10:5)

1. What thoughts, people or activities does your mind tend to
   wander to during prayer? Is there anything like magazines,
   television or books that you can decrease or eliminate in order
   to "take captive" your thoughts?
2. Are there arguments of doubt and disbelief in your mind?
   What Scriptures can you find that would demolish each doubt?
3. What do you do before going to bed every night? The three
   disciplines of meditation, study and solitude can be practiced
   right before falling asleep. Instead of reading a book, read a
   Bible passage and meditate on how it applies to your heart.
   Then "be still" on your bed and listen for God's lullaby.

Your Traveling Companion

Confess to God the things that cause your mind to wander away
from Him. Ask, *Show me the things that I chose to think of more than
You. Help me to make every thought obedient to Your Son.*

Chapter Six

CELEBRATING A CHILD'S STRENGTHS

"What do you want to be when you grow up?" a man asked ten-year-old Josiah.

"I don't know, God hasn't told me yet," he replied.

As I listened to this conversation, I silently prayed, *Thank You, Lord. Maybe my son is getting it after all!*

When I was about the age of nine, I decided that I wanted to become a nurse. My mother had been ill for as long as I could remember, so I guess I felt destined to be some sort of caregiver my entire life. I pursued this dream throughout my school years and prepared to enter medical school. But when I became pregnant my second semester of college, my career came to a screeching halt.

I obviously hadn't planned on becoming a mother at eighteen, but I wasn't sure I wanted to be one at any age. My new husband was struggling with finding his purpose in life, which made it worse for me, since my own dreams had been shattered. *I knew what I wanted to be when I grew up. I just wish he would figure it out for himself.* It wasn't until we both began to surrender our desires, hopes and dreams to the Lord that we could begin to find out God's plan and purpose for our lives—both separately and as husband and wife. Our goals and careers didn't matter as much anymore, since we wanted to "[resolve] to know nothing . . . except Jesus Christ and him crucified" (1 Corinthians 2:2). Our struggles with finding what we wanted to be when "we grew up" began to fade. "This relationship with God then feeds our purposes in life without our fussing and straining too hard to discover or achieve them. The more fully we come to know God, the more clear his purposes become to us."[1]

We didn't want our children to have to struggle with the same sins we did, but to come to know God's will for each of their lives. Our long-term goals for our children didn't focus on what college they attended or what careers they chose. Instead, we concentrated on centering their moral and emotional characters on God. Therefore, whatever skills or abilities they had would be used to glorify God, whether that meant inside or outside the church. That's why I felt thrilled when Josiah said he was waiting to hear from God on what to do when he grew up.

God's Plans for Your Child

Acts 17:26 tells us, "From one man he made every nation of men, that they should inhabit the whole earth; and he determined the times set for them and the exact places where they should live." God placed our children in our home because He knew that Tim and I could help fulfill His plans for each of them.

As I mentioned in Chapter 1, this Scripture has been fulfilled in my childhood experience. My mother's illness kept her away from church a lot. Because my father was a lay preacher, I found myself stepping into the role of a "pastor's wife." Teaching Sunday school, cleaning the church building, preparing communion, counseling a hurting person and making calls to the sick were all part of my life from a very young age. Little did I know that someday my own husband would become a pastor. Of course, God knew the best training ground for me and determined the exact place and time to fulfill His plan.

Realizing that God had placed me in my particular family freed me from bitterness and hurt. I shared this with a friend who dealt with severe abuse from her childhood. The reality that God stood by her all those years, waiting for her to turn to Him, lifted her burden of hatred toward her parents. As with me, it freed her from past hurts. Not only did she drop her dependency on antidepressants, she also began to pray for her parents' salvation. But the biggest joy she found in this biblical truth was the freedom to love her own children. No longer could they blame her for the mistakes she had already made with them. Now she could forgive herself, repent of her mistakes and know that God had given her those children so they would turn to Him.

We can also see God's plan being fulfilled in our children's personalities. I like to think of the emotional characteristics and intellectual abilities of a child as the pearls that must be strung together in order for him to be a whole person in God. For instance, Josiah's moody temperament sometimes drives me crazy. His love and patience for younger children often cloud his judgment when Tim and I are correcting one of the other kids. And of course, his random learning style, creativeness and messiness tell a lot about his personality. But string all these together and it is easy to see God's plan for our son.

If that man asked Josiah today what he wanted to be when he grew up, his answer would now have more direction for his future. He sees the Lord leading him into youth ministry and writing and illustrating children's books. As Tim and I have learned to steer Josiah's individuality toward God, we see His purpose forming in our son. Josiah continues to rejoice more all the time. He keeps his opinions to himself until more appropriate times. Working with the youth in our church has helped him understand the importance of directing and disciplining young children. And much to my delight, the more he learns to harness his creativity, the more organized he becomes. The pearls are beginning to connect.

Sometimes a hobby or interest can be a sign of God's bigger plans for your child. Joshua always had a fascination with airplanes. He read books and magazines and played computer games about flying. When he entered high school he took aviation courses and began flying lessons. We allowed him to test his wings (no pun intended) by taking a job at a major airline. Joshua soon realized that God's plan for him did not include commercial piloting, but perhaps missionary aviation. I laughed one day when I attended an air show with my teenage son. When he was younger he spoke of engines and wingspans at such arenas. Now he looked for cargo room and the capability to land in hard-to-reach areas. As God directed Joshua's heart to find His purpose, my son's interests changed.

Growing up means that a child begins to adapt to life and reality. He learns that there are certain parameters that he must function within if he wants to survive or live a "normal" life. As Christian parents, the boundaries we set for our children should teach them that their very existence comes from God. "For in him we live and move and have our being" (Acts 17:28). We point them toward the Lord and hem them in so that they realize that God has a plan for their lives. As our children grow up, those qualities that God knit into them will help them to adapt to His reality for their lives. The spiritual disciplines, such as fasting, service and celebration, can help us discover the "pearls" in our child's life and string them together.

Fasting

This discipline is often misunderstood and misused. There are some who, because of fear and fleshly weakness, feel they cannot participate in fasting. Others try to use fasting to manipulate God to fulfill their own desires. The main purpose for fasting, however, is to center our hearts on God. When we focus on Him, we can see our own hearts more clearly. Fasting for children means abstaining not only from food at times, but also from entertainment or pleasures. Setting aside such things as television, toys or sweets allows them to learn Paul's admonition, "Since, then, you have been raised with Christ, set your hearts on things above, where Christ is seated at the right hand of God. Set your minds on things above, not on earthly things" (Colossians 3:1-2).

Before Birth

❤ Meditate on Isaiah 58. The kind of fasting the Lord requires is to share our food with the hungry and the poor. I take this to mean spiritual food as well as physical food. "Then Jesus declared, 'I am the bread of life. He who comes to me will never go hungry, and he who believes in me will never be thirsty' " (John 6:35).

❤ I have fasted for short periods while pregnant (usually in my second trimester), perhaps skipping a meal or two and drinking plenty of water or fresh fruit juice. Check with your doctor before entering a fast during pregnancy.

❤ Withdraw for a time from things that distract you (such as television, magazines or hobbies) and spend that time in prayer for your unborn child. Ask God to reveal things that are hidden in your heart such as fear, anxiousness or pride.

❤ Use your pregnancy as an opportunity to cleanse you from unhealthy eating habits, such as caffeine or sugar intake.

Infancy to Preschool: Newborn to Age 5

❤ Even if you are nursing, it may be OK to fast; check with your doctor. Again, drink plenty of water or fresh fruit juice. "Blow the trumpet in Zion, declare a holy fast, call a sacred assembly. Gather the people, consecrate the assembly; bring together the elders, gather the children, those nursing at the breast" (Joel 2:15-16).

❤ When our kids were small and Tim and I fasted, we didn't ask them to fast unless we clearly knew God led us to fast as a family. When we fasted as a church, we tried to fulfill the above passage in Joel by making their meals very light and simple. But we included the children in all prayer and fellowship, instead of separating them from the group.

❤ By the age of two, children are fascinated by television and audio tapes, which can be great teaching tools. If you use these regularly, periodically take a break and read to your child or have an additional quiet time.

Early Childhood: Ages 6-8

💙 Read to your child the story of Daniel in the royal court of Babylon (Daniel 1). My boys loved our "Daniel fasts." We would skip desserts or have vegetarian lunches. Then we would discuss how we sometimes get really caught up in what we eat and how eating healthy can help us serve God better.

💙 Set aside a favorite toy or book or game for a time period. Talk with your child about why he likes this particular item so much. This is a great time to teach them that they can ask God what to do with their time.

💙 Memorize with your child First Corinthians 10:31: "So whether you eat or drink or whatever you do, do it all for the glory of God." Discuss with him the meaning of this Scripture and help him think of ways to apply it in his own life.

Middle Years: Ages 9-12

💙 Take "breaks" from the world for the purpose of focusing on God. Agree as a family not to watch television for a period of time. Spend time in prayer during the hour you might have been watching a favorite program. Be careful not to "reward" your children with television immediately after your "fast" ends.

💙 Fasting can be a means of seeking forgiveness. A child skipping a meal to spend time praying and thinking about an error he has committed can help soften a child's heart. We tried not to make this seem like punishment, but a time for the child to humble himself before God. "Blessed are those who mourn, for they will be comforted" (Matthew 5:4).

💙 Determine what acts of the sinful nature (Galatians 5:19-21) are obvious in your child. Ask God to show you things that your child could "fast" from in order to replace such things with the fruit of the Spirit (5:22-23). Although we saw that Joshua's interest in flying was part of God's plan, we could also sense the temptation of pride and idolatry in this area. So occasionally we had him withdraw from the aviation magazines or the flight simulation computer games in order to seek God.

❤ About this age kids tend to get "obsessed" with the latest trends. For girls, it might be beads, crafts or hair accessories. Boys usually get stuck on sports, cars or skateboarding. Teach them the principle of Ecclesiastes 7:18, "The man who fears God will avoid all extremes," so that there will be less need to "fast" from such things later.

❤ At this stage, especially around twelve, children can start to participate in a full-fledged fast of only water for a few days. Direct their fasting to Isaiah 58, encouraging them to pray for the hungry and for the suffering church. After their fast, direct them in ways of service for others.

Service

Each child has skills and abilities ready to develop into gifts and talents. Since God knits together a child in his mother's womb (Psalm 139:13), these aptitudes are part of the tapestry. The closer we come to God, the clearer His plans in our lives become. And since the Scriptures tell us that whatever we do in "word or deed" must be done "in the name of the Lord Jesus," the eventual intent of testing a child's talents is to point him to fulfilling this purpose. Whatever career or job position they choose later in life should stem from the desire to follow God's plan.

Up until now this book has primarily focused on the greatest commandment—to love God with all our hearts. While we want our children to grow into responsible adults with a strong work ethic and good habits, part of our ultimate goal should also be for them to obey the second greatest commandment—"Love your neighbor as yourself" (Mark 12:31).

The discipline of service teaches a child responsibility, leads him to discover his talents and encourages him to lay down his life for others (John 15:13). Since we have always had an open-door policy in our home, service was a natural part of our lives. It's a rare child that says, "Hey, I'll share my room and give up my toys and time with my parents." Here are some ways we helped our children practice the discipline of service.

Before Birth

♥ While you're pregnant, it's tempting to withdraw from other people. Look for opportunities to develop the discipline of service in your own life.

♥ Follow Jesus' example by "washing the feet" of others (13:3-17). Years ago when it seemed most of the kids in our church were under two, "washing feet" included holding a crying baby, changing diapers or whatever a mother needed. One day out of desperation, one mother nursed another's infant while she baby-sat the child.

♥ Learn to serve in humility by not letting your right hand know what your left hand is doing.

> Be careful not to do your "acts of righteousness" before men, to be seen by them. If you do, you will have no reward from your Father in heaven.
>
> So when you give to the needy, do not announce it with trumpets, as the hypocrites do in the synagogues and on the streets, to be honored by men. I tell you the truth, they have received their reward in full. But when you give to the needy, do not let your left hand know what your right hand is doing, so that your giving may be in secret. Then your

Father, who sees what is done in secret, will reward you. (Matthew 6:1-4)

❤ Learn to be served. One of the hardest things for me to learn was to allow others to help me. But like Peter, who didn't want Jesus to wash his feet, I had to humble myself in submission to others.

Infancy to Preschool: Newborn to Age 5

❤ When a child can carry something in his hands without tumbling over, you can teach him to pick up his toys and help around the house. Make a game of it by singing or racing to pick up the toys.

❤ As he grows, give him more responsibility according to his capabilities. Children who are taught to serve grow in confidence and competence. Helping my father clean the church at the age of five gave me a joy I can still remember. I'm sure he went behind me and checked the bathrooms I scrubbed and pews I dusted, but as my confidence grew so did my skill.

❤ Look for opportunities to serve with your child in the community without receiving anything in return—bake cookies for neighbors, help out at a local shelter, visit the elderly.

Early Childhood: Ages 6-8

❤ Set the example of serving without reward. I have always been an active volunteer at my children's school, but I often spent more time in classrooms other than my children's. Of course, in my heart I wanted to be with my own kids, but I felt that God called me to serve elsewhere.

❤ Demonstrate to your child the power of learning that "the last will be first, and the first will be last" (Matthew 20:16). Encourage them to let others choose the games they will play or let someone else have the last cookie.

♥ At this age chores can begin to include taking out trash, feeding a pet, making a bed, cleaning a bathroom or dusting the furniture. It takes patience to teach a child these things. It's easier sometimes to do it yourself, but the end results in your child's life are worth it.

♥ Make serving fun. A little game I learned from a teacher helped my kids have a good attitude about cleaning up after a particular messy activity. Give each child a different math equation, like 2 + 3, depending on their skill level. (It was a challenge coming up with tough problems for the really "brainy" kids.) The children solve the problem, then race to pick up the same number of pieces of trash as the solution to the problem (in this case, 5). The room is filled with laughter and cleaned up in no time.

♥ Once your child grows skillful in a particular chore, have him apply the new skill to help others. For example, taking care of a neighbor's pet or sweeping and dusting the home of a sick person in the church helps children see that their skills can be used outside the home.

Middle Years: 9-12

♥ As you teach your child to serve, closely and prayerfully watch for things that perk his interests. They may be the very skills God knitted into him for later service. Mowing an elderly woman's yard could lead to running a lawn care business. Enjoying telling others about Jesus could lead to mission work.

♥ Tim and I didn't believe in paying our children for performing chores. We wanted them to have the same attitude of Jesus, so we taught them this passage: "So you also, when you have done everything you were told to do, should say, 'We are unworthy servants; we have only done our duty' " (Luke 17:10). Helping the family and church was the duty of all of us. We gave our children money according to their expenditure needs and according to how the Lord provided.

♥ Teach children to tithe to the Lord. In addition to tithing, we practice "gleaning" in our house and church body. At Christmas time we make "poor boxes." Throughout the year our change and rebate money goes into the box. Then at the end of the year, we pour all the boxes together (no one is allowed to count so everyone's reward is seen in heaven, not by men). We then send the money wherever the Lord leads—Bibles for missionaries, prison ministries, relief agencies—each year it seems to go somewhere new.

♥ Teach your child to serve others in small ways, like helping a sibling with chores or picking up trash on the church or school grounds. Richard Foster says, "True service finds it almost impossible to distinguish the small from the large service. Where a difference is noted, the true servant is often drawn to the small service, not out of false modesty, but because he genuinely sees it as the more important task."[2]

♥ By this stage you probably can recognize your child's intellectual strengths and skills. As you recognize these skills, find ways to point your child into service for the Lord. For instance, Josiah's artistic abilities were strong from the time he was very little. By the time he was twelve, we were asking him to draw and design bulletins, posters and activity sheets for church or Sunday school. Joshua had leadership qualities, so we began to place him in small leadership positions at church. Even if it is not part of God's plan for your child to choose full-time ministry, his skills can still be used for the Lord.

Celebration

The Bible tells us that the joy of the LORD is our strength (Nehemiah 8:10). The discipline of celebration motivates us to work at the other disciplines. Jesus was able to endure the cross because of the joy set before Him (Hebrews 12:2). I often tell struggling parents, "This too will pass." But I also encourage them to not let the cup pass before God has finished the work of the cross in their child's life. I know from experience that there is joy on the other side of pain. It is through trials that God refines us. The Scriptures tell us,

> Consider it pure joy, my brothers, whenever you face trials of many kinds, because you know that the testing of your faith develops perseverance. Perseverance must finish its work so that you may be mature and complete, not lacking anything. (James 1:2-4)

Around our house when something goes wrong, we often say, "Hey, consider it *pure joy!*" It helps us to stop and think about what God might be trying to tell us and ends a lot of grumbling.

Love, Obedience, Joy

I recall singing a song as a child with a chorus that said, "I'm so very happy, I've got the love of Jesus in my heart." Love produces obedience as Jesus stated, "If you love me, you will obey what I command" (John 14:15). In turn, obedience produces happiness. You may have heard the saying, "An obedient child is a happy child." Therefore, it stands to reason that if we desire our homes to be full of joy we must expect obedience from our children. The circle, however, comes back to love. We don't want our children to live in fear, but to obey out of love. Teaching our children to love God with all their heart, soul, mind and strength will produce obedience and in turn a reason to celebrate.

As your child grows and begins to discover his interests and talents, remember the goal is to love God with all his strength. Teach your child to give thanksgiving to God for those strengths. Celebrate the failures as well as the victories. We tend to celebrate A's on a report card or a home run at a baseball game. Teaching children, however, to find joy in their struggles and failures as well as their successes and triumphs helps them to love God with all their energy, no matter how weak or how strong.

Before Birth

❤ Learn to laugh at yourself. Don't take yourself too seriously. Celebration helps us to realize that we are fallible and we need God's help. This is especially helpful to remember when those "beached whale" feelings start to sneak up on you.

❤ Make a list of all the things and people that make you feel thankful. Write a note or tell those people why you are thankful for them.

❤ Do something fun without indulging the flesh. We can become weary and it's healing to spend time relaxing and enjoying life. "Be at rest once more, O my soul, for the LORD has been good to you" (Psalm 116:7).

Infancy to Preschool: Newborn to Age 5

❤ The birth of a child is indeed a celebration in itself. Abraham and Sarah named their son Isaac ("he laughs") because he brought "laughter" to their hearts (Genesis 17:19).

❤ Try to start each day with song and rejoicing. Teach your child from the start to give each day to the Lord. Always incorporate thanksgiving and rejoicing in the Quiet Time Box routine. Although Josiah tended to be melancholy, he raised his hands to the sky and said, "Pays the Lawd!" (Praise the Lord) during our quiet times.

❤ Celebration gives us perspective on our problems. As your child begins to explore his world, bumps and bruises will be part of his daily life. Whenever possible, teach your child to laugh and not to complain. Of course there will be tears, but point your child to trust God during these small scrapes. He will learn to carry that attitude over as he gets older and the trials get tougher. When a little one falls down, I'll often tease (after I've checked for blood and broken bones) by saying, "Let's check the floor. Did you crack the floor?" The tears usually stop immediately and the child starts to giggle. We then praise God that everyone is OK—including the floor.

❤ Delight in your child's creativity. Allow them to explore with their imaginations—to dream dreams and to see visions (Acts 2:17). Four-year-old Joshua loved to pretend to be John the Baptist. He would wrap a brown bath towel around himself, point his finger and shout, "You brood of vipers! Who told you to flee the coming wrath!" Then he would proceed to lower his two-year-old brother to the floor as if to baptize him in the Jordan River.

Early Childhood: Ages 6-8

❤ Allow your children to be noisy sometimes. Teach them that, as Ecclesiastes 3:4 says, there is "a time to weep and a time to laugh, a time to mourn and a time to dance." My children's friends loved coming over to our house because they could be noisy and get the carpets dirty. But they also knew that there were times of quiet reflection.

❤ Children learn through play and through play they develop interests and skills. Provide them with a wide range of things to explore and learn with such as arts and crafts, stories, building blocks, dolls, cars and trucks. Try not to distinguish between "girl" and "boy" toys. Josiah loved to play with dolls and hated cars at this age. It wasn't long before he set his "babies" aside and started asking to help teach the younger kids in Sunday school.

❤ Celebrate when your child learns a new task. For example, have a shoe-tying party when your child learns to tie his own shoes. Pull out everyone's shoes and let him show off his new skill. Then stop and thank the Lord for helping your child with this accomplishment.

❤ Demonstrate thankfulness to your child for expressions of love. One day, while I visited a friend, her six-year-old daughter ran in with a fist full of dandelions. The mother screeched, "Get those nasty things away. I am allergic to those weeds!" The little girl walked away brokenhearted. God draws us with loving-kindness and we should do the same with our children (Jeremiah 31:3).

Middle Years: 9-12

❤ Make events and achievements times of celebration and thanksgiving to the Lord. As Philippians 4:4 says, "Rejoice in the Lord always. I will say it again: Rejoice!" This passage is usually quoted to encourage someone who feels sad or struggling. But to rejoice always means to give God glory in all circumstances; good or bad.

❤ Instill and celebrate a godly "self-esteem" in your child. Secular ideas about having "good self-esteem" and seeing oneself in a positive light are human-centered and go against what Jesus taught. Did Jesus think badly of Himself when He told the rich ruler, "Why do you call me good? . . . No one is good—except God alone" (Mark 10:18)? An unhappy child becomes self-focused on whether his abilities are "good enough." A happy child realizes that his talents come from God and does not focus on self but on Him.

❤ About this stage, many children start wanting to play a musical instrument. Like all areas of his life, encourage your child to pray and seek God's will. When our two youngest sons both picked up instruments in fifth grade, I was delighted that they wanted to worship God in this way. (Trust me—the squeals and squawks of instruments is a "this too will pass" thing!) Keep encouraging your child with the following passage:

Praise the LORD.
Praise God in his sanctuary;
    praise him in his mighty heavens.
Praise him for his acts of power;
    praise him for his surpassing greatness.
Praise him with the sounding of the trumpet,
    praise him with the harp and lyre,
praise him with tambourine and dancing,
    praise him with the strings and flute,
praise him with the clash of cymbals,
    praise him with resounding cymbals.
Let everything that has breath praise the LORD.
Praise the LORD. (Psalm 150:1-6)

♥   Our family has chosen not to celebrate our holidays and
    birthdays in the manner of our culture. Since our main goal for
    our children was to teach them to deny themselves as Christ
    commanded, it felt hypocritical spending days celebrating self.
    We didn't want to be like the Israelites who built a golden calf
    and declared a "festival to the LORD" (Exodus 32:5) when in
    reality they celebrated self. So we found ways, like making the
    poor boxes, to make those times true celebrations toward God.

♥   Celebrate finished accomplishments. Don't allow your child to
    give up on commitments, activities or homework lessons. There
    will be circumstances that may dictate a change of course, but
    whenever possible teach your child to keep his word even when
    it hurts (Psalm 15:4).

♥   Teach your child to do "everything without complaining or
    arguing." Encourage him to respond to homework, chores,
    school lunch menus—everything—with joy and thanksgiving,
    so that he "shines like [a star]" (Philippians 2:14-15).

Although motherhood wasn't originally part of my life goals, it became a major part of God's purpose in my life. Raising my children to love God became my *lifetime* goal. Although Tim is a pastor and writer, he knows raising his sons for the Lord is a high priority in his life. About the time Joshua entered high school, we experienced a time of dryness in our ministry and walk with the Lord, which I believe God brings sometimes to purify our hearts and motives. During this time Tim spent a lot time with the boys, reasoning and instructing them in God's Word. Although the boys had many friends, they had no "best friends" and Tim became that for them. He went places and did things with them that he never would have had time for if he had been busy with his own work.

Almost immediately after Joshua graduated, God brought a renewed spirit and direction in our lives. Tim and I believe that God allowed this dark time not only to test our hearts, but also to keep us centered on raising our two youngest boys for Him. They are now well on their way to understanding what it means to walk with God independent of Mom and Dad. As our children "grow up into him who is the Head, that is, Christ" (Ephesians 4:15), they will discover the strengths and talents God has given them so that they may fulfill the following passage: "If anyone speaks, he should do it as one speaking the very words of God. If anyone serves, he should do it with the strength God provides, so that in all things God may be praised through Jesus Christ. To him be the glory and the power for ever and ever. Amen" (1 Peter 4:11).

The Narrow Path

Scriptural reading: Mark 9:35

Spiritual Guides

Nothing is clearer from the New Testament than that the Lord Jesus expects us to take the low position of servant. This is not just an extra obligation, which we may or may not assume as we please. It is the very heart of that new relation-

ship which the disciple is to take up with respect to God and
to his fellows if he is to know fellowship with Christ and any
degree of holiness in his life. (Roy Hession, *The Calvary
Road*)

Light on the Path

This is how we know what love is: Jesus Christ laid down his
life for us. And we ought to lay down our lives for our brothers. (1 John 3:16)

Jesus knew that the Father had put all things under his power,
and that he had come from God and was returning to God; so
he got up from the meal, took off his outer clothing, and
wrapped a towel around his waist. After that, he poured water into a basin and began to wash his disciples' feet, drying
them with the towel that was wrapped around him. (John
13:3-5)

1. What things do you hang on to in your life that would be hard
   to lay down for someone else? Could you "fast" from any of
   these things?
2. Jesus could be a servant because of the confidence He had in
   God. What things keep you from having confidence in Christ
   and as a result hinder you from serving others?
3. How can you serve someone by practicing the discipline of
   celebration?

Your Traveling Companion

Ask God, *Open my eyes and heart to see who You want me to serve.*

Chapter Seven

~ ~ ~ ~ ~ ~ ~ ~ ~ ~ ~ ~ ~ ~ ~

A CHILD'S SOUL: GOD'S CHERISHED POSSESSION

J osiah says he doesn't want to come home," my friend Pam informed me over the phone.

"Excuse me? Did you say that my four-year-old doesn't want to come home?" I asked, puzzled.

"Yep," she laughed. "He won't get out of the Jacuzzi."

Josiah had spent the night with some friends from church. Their apartment complex had a pool and a hot tub, which apparently my pre-schooler enjoyed. Since the day our little angel was born, he seemed a little more fleshly than most children. Now remember, this is the same kid who Jesus had to visit *personally* to help him give up the comfort of the pacifier.

Josiah always seemed to have his little mind set on what the "sinful nature . . . desires" (Romans 8:5). We tried not to "baby" him, even though he was the youngest, but he still liked to focus on his flesh. At the age of three he got a bad virus which lasted over a week. We tried everything to help him get over it, especially prayer. Josiah, however, refused to pray with us to ask God to help him. Finally almost at the point of dehydration, he cried, "I want to die!" Can you imagine how it felt to hear a three-year-old say such a thing?

At that point I gently encouraged him to pray, then I walked out of the room. Tim and I asked God to touch his little heart and break his stubbornness. Soon we heard the shuffle of footed pajamas, "Mama, Daddy, will you pray with me?" Of course we prayed with our son and Josiah grew well almost immediately. When I refused to give in to his pouting, he changed his attitude, which brought healing to his body. As Proverbs 17:22 says, "A cheerful heart is good medicine, but a crushed spirit dries up the bones."

God's Plan for Your Child

We know that God knits characteristics into each child before birth (Psalm 139:13) and determines the exact times and places for each person to be born in order to spur us on to cry out to Him (Acts 17:26). Therefore, a child's basic likes and dislikes, individual personality and purpose in life were woven together in the womb in order to draw him toward following God.

The line between the heart, the center of our desires, and the soul, the center of our will, is very thin. As we impress the commandments of God on our children's hearts and minds, we divide their desires and motives. As Hebrews 4:12 says, "For the word of God is living and active. Sharper than any double-edged sword, it penetrates even to dividing soul and spirit, joints and marrow; it judges the thoughts and attitudes of the heart."

In the beginning man's heart was full of love for his Creator, and his mind and strength were in obedience to God's will. Man's soul was satisfied to walk with God. Then the serpent tempted man with discontentment and Satan touched man's soul through the flesh. Adam was no longer gratified by submitting to God's purpose for him. Satan used the flesh to reach the soul's desires. Everything we have looked at up to this point influences a child's thoughts and actions as we try to steer his heart toward God. We have looked at how to use the outward to reach the inward part of a child. In this chapter, we will discuss the importance of trusting the Lord with our children's souls, the hidden place where a man makes decisions of the will.

We must realize that while we may win the heart of a child and influence his mind, ultimately his soul belongs to the Lord. As Ezekiel 18:4 states, "For every living soul belongs to me, the father as well as the son—both alike belong to me. The soul who sins is the one who will die." The context of this passage tells how the people of Israel blamed their forefathers for "sour grapes"—in other words, their sins and misery. God steps in and says that each man is accountable for his own sins. Each man must make the decision for himself whether or not to obey God. Parents can do their best to influence their children, but in the end each individual child must make the decision to love God with all of his soul.

The first step we take in helping our children to love God with all their souls is to see them plainly. We have to see each child's weaknesses and strengths honestly. Parents must take the time to reason with their children to help them see their hearts clearly. God revealed man's heart after the fall by asking questions like, "Where are you?" and "Who told you that you were naked?" (Genesis 3:9-11). While we laughed at Josiah's Jacuzzi incident, Tim and I realized that it was a sign of how much he wanted his flesh soothed. We connected it to the time he wanted attention when he was sick and refused to pray. Yet, we never disciplined him for "not wanting to come home" or said, "How can you be so fleshly?" but asked God how we might help Him change our son.

Often parents respond to their children's behavior by reacting way too fast. They set strict standards, causing children to conform to please their parents. On the other hand, some parents ignore their children's sins and faults because they want to keep peace. (Many working mothers, for example, have told me that because they feel guilty for being away from their children, they often allow bad behaviors to go unchallenged.)

Saving a child's soul is a lifetime process. God had a plan for His children after they disobeyed. But it took several thousand years for man to be ready for Christ. God doesn't look at us and say, "They're born again, so everything is fine." He perseveres in molding and perfecting us, and we must do the same with our children.

If Tim and I had one main goal for our children it would be for them to fall in love with God and depend totally on Him. It is very important to teach children independence—or, more precisely, dependence on God rather than parents. As Tim and I pointed our children away from us and toward their heavenly Father, God moved on their souls. We prayed for God's direction in our children's lives as we worked on their hearts and minds and honestly admitted what motivated each of them. We looked for ways to help them change their desires into godly ones. Then God could reach down into their souls.

As parents, we have a tendency to encourage our children to be dependent on us. We draw attention to ourselves and want to feel that our kids need us. Teaching our children the spiritual disciplines points them toward God and away from us. This is part of our commitment to follow Luke 14:26: "If anyone comes to me and does not hate his father and mother, his wife and children, his brothers and sisters—yes, even his own life—he cannot be my disciple." Tim and I strive to develop a "godly hatred" for our children—in other words, the love we have for our children has to come fully from God, the source of love. If God is love, any love we have apart from Him is selfish and full of favoritism (1 John 4:16).

Over the years we dealt with Josiah's longing for the comforts of this world by teaching him to practice the spiritual disciplines. Whenever we sensed that Josiah was overly dependent on us, we pointed him toward the Lord. If his flesh rose up, we found ways to deal with it through guidance, submission and prayer. We went through many battles trying to help Josiah trust God with all his heart.

On the night before my husband was scheduled to lead a seminar, thirteen-year-old Josiah developed a severe sinus infection which pressed on his brain and hospitalized him. Tim contemplated canceling the seminar, but as a family we felt that was not God's will. Josiah encouraged us to go to the seminar. Tim and I left the hospital wondering if we would ever see our son alive again. The doctors called me during the seminar to sign the permission papers for emergency brain surgery.

When I arrived at the hospital I noticed a pile of tissues on Josiah's bed. He had obviously been crying. The doctors had told Josiah, without the presence of his parents, that he would probably die. I immediately wanted to extend my motherly claws. Josiah saw the fire in his mother's eyes and reassured me, "It's OK. I had a long talk with God. I told Him that I am ready to die." It was hard to believe that this was the same little boy who didn't even want to pray to God years before. While his dad taught others how to give all to Christ, our son had made the choice to give his soul to God.

There are certainly no guarantees that a child will respond to God's touch on his soul. When our oldest left home, the last thing he said was "God is not enough," knowing it would hurt his father more than anything. The greatest desire in his dad's life is to find complete satisfaction with God alone—in his life and his children's.

Even if you do all the things suggested in this book, your child may still decide not to follow the Lord. Tim and I do not place our hope in what we *did* and *didn't do* with our children. When I look at my own actions, I feel hopeless because I see the areas in which I failed. Therefore, my hope must remain in the Lord.

> But the eyes of the LORD are on those who fear him,
>> on those whose *hope* is in his unfailing love,
> to deliver them from death
>> and keep them alive in famine.
> We wait in *hope* for the LORD;
>> he is our help and our shield.
> In him our hearts rejoice,
>> for we trust in his holy name.
> May your unfailing love rest upon us, O LORD,
>> even as we put our *hope* in you.
>> (Psalm 33:18-22, italics added)

I've learned that placing my hope in God rather than my parenting techniques allows room for the Father to work. While our oldest went through his rebellion stage, I had a tendency to try to influence his heart in my own strength. For example, sometimes when Tim would attempt to deal with areas of sin in our son's life, I would protect Mark and "look for the positive" rather than allow the discipline to do its work. After he left home, I stepped aside and began to watch God work in our two remaining sons. I worked at becoming slow to speak and quick to listen (James 1:19) so God could draw out their hearts and motives. As I watched His hand mold and fashion my children, I felt humbled and encouraged, and I desired to allow God more room to work in their lives.

In the other chapters I listed things you can do to encourage your children to love God with all their hearts, minds and strength, but I have no bullet points in this chapter that can make a soul (the hidden place of the will) love God. I don't believe a parent has the right to touch their children's souls. Trying to influence the soul only makes a child live religion, not a relationship with God. As we find ways to fashion their hearts, fill their minds and encourage their strengths, we make room for God to reach down and touch their souls. All the spiritual disciplines impact the whole child, but the last three—submission, guidance and simplicity—have a direct effect on the soul.

Submission

As I grew up, my mother often said, "If a black sheep crossed the yard and I said it was white—it is white." I was not to argue or correct her in any way. When my children reached the stage where they began to question my judgments, I felt tempted to use the same lecture with them. But I didn't want my children to submit to me "just because I said so." I wanted them to obey out of love for me and for God. As Jesus said, "If you love me, you will obey what I command" (John 14:15).

Many of us have experienced a negative view of submission in our families or churches. True biblical submission releases us from the bondage of self. It is the releasing of our desires to the will of another. Teaching our children to practice the spiritual discipline of submission means encouraging them to turn their wills over to God's will. It is a transformation of the mind and heart so that the soul gives way to obedience.

> Therefore, I urge you, brothers, in view of God's mercy, to offer your bodies as living sacrifices, holy and pleasing to God—this is your spiritual act of worship. Do not conform any longer to the pattern of this world, but be transformed by the renewing of your mind. Then you will be able to test and approve what God's will is—his good, pleasing and perfect will. (Romans 12:1-2)

Dealing with our children's hearts, minds and strengths helps them to become living sacrifices. Then they can test God's perfect will for their lives and submit their souls to it. Parents must live a life of self-denial in order to set the example for their children. Children should see their parents, while standing up for the truth, giving up opinions, desires and attitudes. The cross means death to self and it's the only way to follow Jesus. "If anyone would come after me, he must deny himself and take up his cross and follow me" (Matthew 16:24).

Living a life of self-denial brings freedom to a child's heart. I grew up feeling that I was never "good enough." As a result, I walked in fear and became a people-pleaser. One day early in our Christian walk I was wallowing in self-pity. Tim asked, "Why are you trying to be so good when it's impossible?" That took me back. *Of course I could be good. I was always told to be a "good girl."* My husband then took me to the Bible and made me read Jesus' words: "As Jesus started on his way, a man ran up to him and fell on his knees before him. 'Good teacher,' he asked, 'what must I do to inherit eternal life?' 'Why do you call me good?' Jesus answered. 'No one is good—except God alone' " (Mark 10:17-18).

Wow, if Jesus said that He wasn't good, why was I trying so hard to be good? It was one of those "the truth will set you free" revelations and I began to work on changing my self-doubts to self-denial. I stopped trying to be perfect and surrendered to Him who is perfect. And I vowed that my children would never have to be "good enough." I admit I still slip back into self-effort and I know that affects my kids. The more we deny ourselves and allow the new self to take over, the more our souls surrender to His will.

When Christ said to take up our crosses daily, He meant that we have to die to our own wills and follow Him. We must make a conscious decision to become crucified with Christ so that He might live through us. "I have been crucified with Christ and I no longer live, but Christ lives in me. The life I live in the body, I live by faith in the Son of God, who loved me and gave himself for me" (Galatians 2:20).

As our children's hearts, minds and strengths come under submission to Christ, their souls become one with Him. When their souls are at rest with God, then they can submit to God and man. Their obedience to their parents flows from a love for God. They may still question us, but they learn to do so respectfully. I've learned, too, that there are times when *parents* must submit to their *children* "out of reverence for Christ" (Ephesians 5:21). Believe it or not, sometimes children are right in a situation. It's not always important for parents to "prove a point." Realizing this fact frees both you and your child from anger and frustration, while promoting open communication and acceptance in the family.

Children who learn to submit to God and their parents without grumbling "shine like stars in the universe" away from home as well (Philippians 2:15). We always taught our children to submit to their teachers and governing authorities, as long as it didn't go against their convictions or the Scriptures. Whenever they came home grumbling about a teacher, we would tell them that they had no idea what she might have dealt with that day. Maybe she had a sick child of her own at home. Or perhaps she didn't feel well herself. We would then stop and pray for us to have love and understanding for the teacher. I cannot tell you how many teachers bragged about our boys' obedience at school. (In fact, they were so obedient, I sometimes wondered if they were talking about *my* children!) As a result, teachers tended to respect our sons' wishes when they refused to participate in something due to their convictions. The same teacher frustrated with Joshua for not writing the "I wish . . ." paper didn't question later when he refused to sing a song that went against his conscience.

Parents must practice the discipline of submission before their children. Seeing their parents submit joyfully and willfully to governing authorities and employers helps children see the fruit of a surrendered life. Mothers who submit to their husbands "as is fitting in the Lord" (Colossians 3:18) instill respect and honor for the father, and in turn for the Heavenly Father. Husbands who love their wives as Christ loved the church (Ephesians 5:25) set an example of submission and service for their children. In his role as a pastor, Tim has tried to set the precedent of serving and submitting to the body. All these examples of submission press on the soul of a child and cause him to submit to others in his own life.

The discipline of submission helps children keep their minds set on obeying God. They can resist temptation because they have learned the power of self-denial. Children who submit willfully purify their hearts before God and He draws near to their souls. "Submit yourselves, then, to God. Resist the devil, and he will flee from you. Come near to God and he will come near to you" (James 4:7-8).

Guidance

When our children have learned how to practice submission, their hearts and minds are ready for the spiritual discipline of guidance. Remember that the soul is the place where a man makes a decision for the Lord. We want our children to willfully choose to allow God to guide them. As they learn to submit their wills to God, their hearts, minds and souls are no longer guided by opinions, emotions or feelings, but by the hand of God.

In the Garden, man gave his soul over to Satan. Now only through repentance can we surrender our souls back to God. As parents, we can guide our children to submit their wills to God so that He can "will and . . . act according to his good purpose" (Philippians 2:13) in their lives. Just a spark of surrender and obedience causes God to move on a soul. We guide our children by steering their hearts and minds toward God, but only He can ultimately cause their souls to surrender. Jesus said, "This is why I told you that no one can come to me unless the Father has enabled him" (John 6:65).

The saints of the Middle Ages traveled their inward journeys with the help of spiritual directors. These were people who led others to the way of holiness because they had walked there themselves. A spiritual director understands that as Christ suffered, we too must suffer. Our sufferings include wrestling with sin in our bodies, facing persecutions and picking up the cross of Christ in our lives. As Romans 8:16-17 states, "The Spirit himself testifies with our spirit that we are God's children. Now if we are children, then we are heirs—heirs of God and co-heirs with Christ, if indeed we share in his sufferings in order that we may also share in his glory." A spiritual director has found the way of the cross to be a joy and longs to lead others there as well.

Parents can fulfill the role of spiritual director in their children's lives, but only if we have learned to pick up our own cross. If we try to direct our children's spiritual lives apart from the cross, we will guide them by our own power into our own religious opinions. This means our children must see us waiting on God and persevering as He guides us into His will. They must see us count it "pure joy" when we face trials (James 1:2).

I recall a time when Tim and I were seeking the Lord for guidance about where we should live. On the way home from an exploratory trip that appeared to be a closed door, I broke into tears of weariness and frustration every few miles. My ten-year-old popped in a music tape which included Twila Paris' song, "Do I Trust You, Lord." At that point, my son had become my spiritual director. I then realized that for the sake of my children, I had to stop and spiritually guide them to follow First Thessalonians 5:16-18: "Be joyful always; pray continually; give thanks in all circumstances, for this is God's will for you in Christ Jesus."

The goal of teaching children the spiritual discipline of guidance is that they eventually will depend on God. We cannot be with our children twenty-four hours a day, seven days a week. They must learn to rely on the Spirit to lead them. If we guide our children's hearts and minds to God when we are with them, it frees their souls to be guided by God when we are apart.

Praying the Promises

Many passages in Scripture promise that God will guide us. I have learned to adopt such passages as prayers for my children—for example:

> *Oh, Lord, instruct my children and teach them in the way they should go; counsel them and watch over them.* (Based on Psalm 32:8)

> *Father, send forth Your light and Your truth, let them guide my sons; let them bring my children to Your holy mountain, to the place where You dwell.* (Based on Psalm 43:3)

> *Lord, guide my sons always; satisfy their needs in a sun-scorched land and strengthen their frame. May they be like a well-watered garden, like a spring whose waters never fail.* (Based on Isaiah 58:11)

> *Father, as my sons acknowledge You in all their ways, make their paths straight.* (Based on Proverbs 3:6)

The greatest tool parents have for guiding their children is the Word of God. The Lord will never ask us to guide our children to do anything that goes against His Word. Remember the commandment to love God with all our heart, mind, soul and strength begins with impressing His laws on our children. Outwardly guiding our children with Scripture opens their hearts to the inward guidance of the Holy Spirit. It is imper-

ative that our children obey not because we said so, but because God's
Word says so.

Joshua, now nineteen, recently told me that his favorite passage
since he was eight or nine is Psalm 119:9-16. When he struggles with
sin or needs guidance from the Lord he meditates on these words:

> How can a young man keep his way pure?
> > By living according to your word.
> I seek you with all my heart;
> > do not let me stray from your commands.
> I have hidden your word in my heart
> > that I might not sin against you.
> Praise be to you, O LORD;
> > teach me your decrees.
> With my lips I recount
> > all the laws that come from your mouth.
> I rejoice in following your statutes
> > as one rejoices in great riches.
> I meditate on your precepts
> > and consider your ways.
> I delight in your decrees;
> > I will not neglect your word.

A passage many parents tend to cling to is Proverbs 22:6: "Train a
child in the way he should go, and when he is old he will not turn from
it." The word "train" in this passage means "start" or "initiate."
Starting our children out in the guidance of God's Word makes room
for God to work on their souls their entire lives.

Simplicity

Along with the psalmist who wrote, "As the deer pants for streams
of water, so my soul pants for you, O God" (Psalm 42:1), we long to
simplify and purify our lives. Tim always encourages me to express
"spiritual truths in spiritual words" (1 Corinthians 2:13), so when I

speak of simplifying our lives, he often says, "You mean *purify* our lives." Tim sees the issue in the light of Jesus' words, "Blessed are the pure in heart, for they will see God" (Matthew 5:8).

I need outward simplicity to help purify my heart, while my husband's purity leads to simplicity. Because we look at this spiritual discipline from different angles, when we deal with our children we balance each other out. I enjoy leading them in simplifying their schedules and belongings so they might purely seek the Lord. Tim strives to purify their hearts so they simplify their lives. Thomas à Kempis speaks of "a pure mind and simple intentions":

> There are two wings that lift a person up from earthly things: simplicity and purity. Simplicity should be our intentions, purity our feelings. Simplicity reaches toward God, purity apprehends and enjoys Him.[1]

Why list simplicity as a discipline of the soul when it seems like an outward discipline? Because the desire for material possessions and for recognition in this world can quickly rob a person of his soul. Jesus made the point with the simple question, "What good is it for a man to gain the whole world, yet forfeit his soul?" (Mark 8:36).

Many Christians believe one can solve the issue of material possessions by saying, "I just put money in its proper perspective." But this attitude sets aside the absoluteness of the command to love God with *all* your heart, soul, mind and strength, because it sees the love of money as something to tone down, rather than something to crucify. Jesus stated clearly that "No one can serve two masters. Either he will hate the one and love the other, or he will be devoted to the one and despise the other. You cannot serve both God and Money" (Matthew 6:24). If we do not hate and despise money, if we do not forsake the desire for it, then we cannot serve God. The practice of simplicity starts with teaching our children Paul's command to the Colossians: "Set your minds on things above, not on earthly things" (Colossians 3:2).

I can be a coupon cutter and bargain hunter with the best of them. But Tim and I have learned that one way to deny self is to buy things only according to God's will, coupon or no coupon. If God chooses to provide for a need, He certainly can afford the regular price. This perspective keeps us from hanging on to our money or buying something just because it's on sale. We strive to trust the Lord to provide all our needs—and once in a while, for my sake, God throws in a bargain!

Like all parents, Tim and I love to see our children happy and we desire to give them everything they want, but our commitment to love them with God's love helps us to see which desires to fulfill and which to deny. Their heavenly Father knows their wants and needs and longs to fill their hearts with joy. Teaching children simplicity helps them to trust God for earthly desires and needs.

When Joshua was seven, his bike was stolen and we were not in a financial position to buy him a new one. For several months, Joshua told us that he asked the Lord for a new bike, but was told he must wait. One morning he announced that God had said that today he would get a bike. (At the time, we had another family of four and a single woman living with us; we could barely afford to put food on the table, let alone buy him a bicycle.) Tim and I discussed how to tell our son that it was not possible to get him a bike at this time. If we had had the faith of a little child, we would have expected the check that arrived in the mail that day. Our ministry received a large donation that covered all our needs—with enough left over for a new bike. Through contentment and a pure heart, Joshua learned, "My God will meet all your needs according to his glorious riches in Christ Jesus" (Philippians 4:19).

Remember Martha and Mary? Practicing simplicity moves us into the balance of *doing* and *being*. Our doing becomes saturated in being in the presence of God. In her book *Simply the Savior*, Nancy Parker Brummett tells readers that Jesus gave us a "to-do list." She points out that Christians are called to "Be doers of the word, and not hearers only" (James 1:22, NKJV). Nancy says, "When we create our to-do lists from the Word, they include tasks like loving one another, encouraging one another, carrying one another's burdens, and serving one another . . . all as Jesus did."[2] When we are guided by the Word, our to-do list contains more relationship-building activities than self-improvement.

The Son of God led a life of service. A life of simplicity will also be one of service. Children can be taught to pray about what activities they should participate in and which ones to skip. Encourage them to have a mind-set of service in everything they do. Then soccer games, band practices, school projects, etc., become chances to serve others and to make the most of every opportunity (Ephesians 5:16). As their hearts are purified then they "will see God" who is the example of service.

Protecting and encouraging our children's souls is a life-long process. A life of self-denial and service opens the door for God to touch their wills and souls. Today Josiah leads a life of service for others and I cannot even imagine him sitting in a Jacuzzi, much less refusing to get out of one. But one thing is certain: he longs to go Home. Weeks after his surgery, Josiah told me he was actually disappointed that he didn't wake up in heaven. My son's soul rejoices in the Lord (Psalm 35:9).

The Narrow Path

Scripture reading: Psalm 62:1-2

Spiritual Guides

> The presence of God is the concentration of the soul's attention on God, remembering that He is always present. . . . The presence of God is, then, the life and nourishment of the soul, which can be acquired with the grace of God. (Brother Lawrence, *The Practice of the Presence of God*)

Light on the Path

> I wait for the LORD, my soul waits, and in his word I put my hope. (Psalm 130:5)

May God himself, the God of peace, sanctify you through and through. May your whole spirit, soul and body be kept blameless at the coming of our Lord Jesus Christ. (1 Thessalonians 5:23)

1. What things hold your attention? How can you simplify your life so that you may enter the presence of God?
2. Do you find it hard to wait on the Lord to work in your life? Ask God to guide you in His Word to the passages that will nourish your soul at this time.
3. What areas in your life have you yet to submit to God? How do these things prevent your "whole spirit, soul and body" from being blameless?

Your Traveling Companion

Pray, *Show me the things that clutter my life and keep be from submitting to You. Guide me in Your Word so that I might become my children's spiritual director.*

Chapter Eight

THE JELL-O YEARS

You awaken one morning and find yourself talking to a stranger. Your sweet little child has suddenly become a horrifying creature. He rarely remembers to bring home his school work. He locks himself out of the house three times in one week. He stirs the spaghetti noodles and asks, "What's for dinner?" One minute he talks to you sweetly and the next your child's personality explodes right before your eyes. You cry, "I want my baby back!"

Somewhere between the ages of eight and thirteen a child enters what my husband lovingly dubbed the "The Jell-O Years"—a time in your child's life when you swear you can actually see his brain wiggle from lack of substance. Tim and I have raised three sons and numerous temporary custody children, mostly preteens; we've become experts at spotting the signs of the Jell-O years.

The behavioral changes that children go through at this age shock many parents, who often resist the transition. Several parents have told me that they eased up on family rules, such as homework and curfews, in hopes of "getting their sweet baby back." This attitude could be disastrous for your child and family. Matthew 11:12 tells us that "The kingdom of heaven has been forcefully advancing, and forceful men take hold of it." At this stage parents must take hold of their child's heart like never before.

By the time most children reach this age, their parents have settled lives with careers, homes and families. Preadolescent children demand less attention and become more independent, giving the deceptive illusion that parents can finally have a life apart from the kids. Preteens can take themselves to a public restroom, make choices from a menu, find a ride to events with friends and develop interests of their own. If you are too busy, you will miss teachable moments to instill spiritual disciplines.

It would be unfair not to provide you with an understanding of preadolescence if I expect you to implement anything in this book. Often this stage is overlooked in parenting books and blended into the early school age and teenage stages. As you strive to practice the spiritual disciplines you might feel like quitting as you reach this stage. Or maybe you're just beginning to see the importance of the disciplines and your preteen is not responding. Understanding how your child grows and changes physically, cognitively, socially, emotionally and spiritually can help you persevere through this stage.

Physically

As in any stage, children follow their own timetables of growth. As much as you would like to put off your daughter starting her menstrual cycle, you cannot control how fast or slow your child matures physically. At this stage parents need to discuss the physical growth taking place with their child. Children should hear from their parents—not their friends—about the changes in their bodies.

A few years ago, my elderly neighbor expressed her concerns over her twelve-year-old granddaughter's drastic mood swings. "Grandma," as all the neighbors call her, lives with her single-parent son and his daughter. Having been through this stage several times with temporary custody daughters, I quickly recognized the signs. "Have you talked to her about starting her period?" I asked. Since she had only a son, Grandma hadn't thought of such a possibility. I encouraged her to buy the supplies needed and to put some in her granddaughters' backpack. Within the week the father knocked on my door to thank me for helping his daughter prepare for this special time in her life.

Boys tend to develop slower than girls at this stage, but their bodies go through changes as well. Girls usually begin puberty between the ages of eight and thirteen, while boys begin somewhere between ten and fourteen. Thoughts of the opposite sex are prevalent as your child moves closer to becoming a teenager. Practicing the spiritual disciplines during this phase of maturity can help your child have peace as his body changes. For instance, meditation on God's Word can steer a child's thoughts toward the Lord and away from the typical preadolescent daydreams.

This is the stage where parents need to begin teaching their children about sex. Encourage your child not to be afraid of confessing any thoughts he may have in regards to this topic. As your child begins to have more questions and understanding in this area, give him Scriptures to meditate on that encourage purity.

My favorite passage for girls is Song of Solomon 8:8-9: "We have a young sister, and her breasts are not yet grown. What shall we do for our sister for the day she is spoken for? If she is a wall, we will build towers of silver on her. If she is a door, we will enclose her with panels of cedar." For boys, I share Psalm 119:9: "How can a young man keep his way pure? By living according to your word."

Around this age we discussed with our boys what the Bible says about relationships with the opposite sex. Using Scripture as our guide we taught our boys to treat "younger women as sisters, with absolute purity" (1 Timothy 5:2). We also impressed on our children the following passage:

> Are you unmarried? Do not look for a wife. But if you do marry, you have not sinned; and if a virgin marries, she has not sinned. But those who marry will face many troubles in this life, and I want to spare you this.
>
> What I mean, brothers, is that the time is short. From now

on those who have wives should live as if they had none. (1
Corinthians 7:27-29)

Our culture pushes dating so early on our children. The desire to be
accepted by the opposite sex is marketed by every possible media. We
taught our children what we felt the Bible said about dating, but reassured them that they would be allowed to date if they so chose. As their
parents, we would set guidelines and boundaries if they chose this
route. Our two younger sons and many of our temporary custody children found this freeing. They no longer had to live up to certain expec-
tations of their friends. Many Christian young people take this same
stand and are uniting for purity.

At the preteen stage, your child will be ready for a more independent
style of quiet time. Provide him with books and devotions that guide
him in the Word. As our children reached twelve or thirteen, Tim began leaving them Scriptures more frequently in order to guide them. I
wrote questions out for the girls and left them verses to encourage them
to practice the discipline of study.

Realize that as your child changes physically he may need more
sleep; his nutritional needs may also increase. He may go on a "feed"
for several days or weeks, then suddenly lose his appetite. His body is
storing up energy for the dramatic growth spurts. Even partial fasts can
help him gain self-control during this phase. Encourage your child to
practice times of solitude and prayer to quiet his heart and mind. Activities and school functions increase for children at this age. Practicing
simplicity removes the excess stimuli that preteens sometimes cannot
handle.

Cognitively

The changes in a child's thinking skills probably scare parents more
than any other change. Suddenly, your child moves toward abstract
thinking. He can reason through situations, memorize and retrieve information, better understand the consequences of behavior and negoti-
ate, or sometimes manipulate, to get what he wants.

Like a child's physical growth, his mental abilities are not yet complete. A child will have growth in one area of thinking but not in another. That's why Tim and I coined the term Jell-O years because a child's thinking process has not quite "set."

This can cause some frustration and challenges for parents. As your child tries to put together meaning and logic, you may find him arguing to prove his points. He may ask the most obvious questions and misunderstand the simplest instructions. A preteen's reasoning is very logical and real to him. Take the time to understand why he thinks the way he does. By being allowed to reason with Tim and me, our children have learned the errors of their thinking and often so have we.

The spiritual discipline of submission becomes a high priority at this stage. Allow your child to respectfully express his feelings, but don't be afraid to say, "We've discussed this enough. You'll just have to trust me on this." We all face times when we don't get the things we desire. Sometimes we must obey God even if we don't understand His ways. Children must learn to submit to their parents. As Proverbs 1:7-8 tells us, "The fear of the LORD is the beginning of knowledge, but fools despise wisdom and discipline. Listen, my son, to your father's instruction and do not forsake your mother's teaching."

Be willing to be misunderstood and disliked once in a while. You'll be your child's worst enemy one minute and his best friend the next. This is especially true with girls. There's no doubt about it, your own feelings will be crushed at times. But work hard not to take everything your child says personally. Realize he longs for independence, yet likes knowing that you're close by. Find ways to show support without coddling too much. Look directly at your child when he speaks to you and show a genuine interest in his ideas, no matter how silly they may seem to you.

Parents must not allow their child's arguments to trap them. Don't avoid conflict at all costs, but don't set up confrontation either. Avoid phrases like, "You always . . ." and "You never. . . ." Teach your child, however, to see the truth in everything. Because of immature cognitive skills, a preteen's logic seems anything but truthful at times and you will often find yourself confused or troubled by his words. For the first time he can think his way around things and experiment with answers and excuses, and he may not always make appropriate choices or realize that he is giving a false impression.

Take the time to ask guided questions that reveal the true motives for his behavior. One of our temporary custody daughters had a tendency to put off her homework until the last minute. Like most preteens, when challenged, she stated reasons beyond her control that caused the delay. Just a few direct questions exposed the fallacies in her excuses and helped her to recognize her problem with procrastination.

Tim often reminds me to remember Ecclesiastes 5:2b: "God is in heaven and you are on earth, so let your words be few." I find it tempting to try to second guess what my children are thinking, which turns them off faster than anything else. Practicing the spiritual disciplines in my own life helps me to control my tongue as I allow the Word of God to guide conversations with my children.

Socially

Walk through any middle school and observe the differences in the students. You will discover that their social maturity varies as much as their height. The changes will vary from grade to grade as well. A student considered "shy" in the sixth-grade may have a leading role in the school play the next year. During this time of wonderful growth and changes, there are many opportunities to practice the discipline of celebration. Always strive to point your child back to the Lord as the Source of his achievements.

Your child will begin to build on the foundation of social skills you taught him and experiment outside your family circle. It's very important to support your child's social arena. Along with the temporary custody children in our home, my children's friends spent a lot of time at our house. We set up an extra computer to draw kids from the neighborhood who needed assistance with homework. Through this ministry, our boys learned to practice the discipline of service.

Participating in church functions becomes a higher priority at this stage. Children want to join in church activities and worship services more frequently. But don't be surprised if they also have times of boredom and discontentment. Practicing worship and service helps a child become socially involved with the church community.

Emotionally

A popular cartoon character, Katy Kaboom, best depicts this growth change in a preteen. One minute she is happily singing and the next angrily exploding. It will seem as if overnight you are suddenly at odds with your child.

Wise parents recognize the turmoil and confusion preadolescent growth brings and allow their child to express his feelings and even pout at times. God lets us air our opinions and feelings. Moses said he didn't want to lead the Israelites out of Egypt. Jeremiah complained to God about the people of Israel. And Elijah ran to the desert in fear for his life.

God allowed these men of old to argue and reason with Him, then explained His will and gave specific instructions on how to fulfill it. We can follow His example by patiently guiding our children to obey and follow God's will and our rules. Parents must accept their child's failures as well as successes and lovingly recognize his feelings as genuine.

Spiritually

During this age children have a distinctive softness toward God. They begin to desire a relationship with Him independent of their parents or Sunday school teachers. Preteens often ask questions like, *Why did God put me here—at this time and place? What are His plans for my life?* Parents may not have satisfying answers for some questions, such as, *Why does God allow people to suffer?* or *Why is there a hell?* Practicing the spiritual disciplines gives children an avenue to discover answers on their own.

No longer does your child focus on Bible stories and characters. Now he wants to know how the stories relate to his life. Don't make the mistake of viewing your child's questioning as a sign of rebellion. See it instead as an opportunity for you to become his spiritual director. When your child asks a question, he is seeking an answer. Guide him in his search.

Your spiritual role in your child's life at this age is somewhat like that of John the Baptist: you are "making way for the Lord" in your child's heart. It's time to level the valleys and mountains in his life, to teach him submission, confession and repentance. Keep eternity in mind in all things. Don't think of daily struggles as battles that will blow over, but as opportunities to teach your child lessons for the future.

Do not err on the side of totally accepting your child no matter what he does. God loves and accepts us as His children, but He does not accept our sin. Teach that there is forgiveness, but there are also consequences to sin and disobedience. Set clear, concise and easily obeyed rules. Don't overlook minor sins or infractions of your guidelines unless they serve the purpose of teaching the concept of God's grace and mercy. God disciplined Moses and kept him from entering the Promised Land even though his sin seemed minor. God and Moses had a close relationship, but Moses still faced the consequences of disobedience.

The preteen years are a time when children seem to get an extra spark for the Lord. They are inquisitive and creative, and because relationships and acceptance mean so much to them, it's very common for them to make a commitment to the Lord. In our ministry, Tim and I have seen many parents confuse an awakening in their child with a decision to give his heart completely to God. In their enthusiasm to seal their child's faith, parents often tend to push for commitments too soon. Parents should provide structure for prayer, worship and personal devotions, but allow their child to experiment, question and internalize his faith at this age. This freedom to test his beliefs will be important during the teen years when he may have to make choices that affect his entire life.

As you begin to enter this stage with your child, you may have a tendency to want to just survive. Yes, there are a lot of "this too will pass" events going on in a preadolescent's life. But you're going to do more than survive—you're going to change. A prepared parent will change for the better and accept this time as a chance to grow closer and more dependent on God. If you choose only to "survive" preadolescence, you will be unprepared and hindered when your child becomes a teenager. You can still control a preteen, but only influence a teenager. The spiritual disciplines are the tools that can help you guide your child to make the decision to follow the Lord's will.

Prayerfully plan ahead how you might react to changes in your child. Think about how you will tell your daughter about her menstrual cycle or your son about sex. How will you feel the first time your child slams the door and says, "Leave me alone!" or "I hate you!"? What guidelines will you set for the types of activities, friends and entertainment your child chooses? How will you respond if he refuses to participate in family worship or attend church? Planning ahead before hitting these roadblocks will help you become the spiritual director your child will need.

The good news about kids is that they are teachable. But you have to be quick on your feet. How many times have you made Jell-O and forgot to put in the fruit? There is just a short window of time when you can mold and pour gelatin. The same is true for your preteen. Timing is crucial. You can hold onto some issues, like not following instructions or forgetting to feed a pet, until a more appropriate time. Issues, however, like breaking curfew or lying may need to be dealt with immediately. God wants your help to pour your child into a special mold, but you have to be ready to hear His instructions.

A prepared parent will look forward to this age with eager anticipation of what God can do in the life of their child. As First Peter 1:13 says, "Prepare your [mind] for action; be self-controlled; set your hope fully on the grace to be given [to] you when Jesus Christ is revealed."

Following the suggestions for practicing the spiritual disciplines can make preadolescence an enjoyable phase. As Christ reveals Himself in your child's life, you will notice the Jell-O fading away. You might wake up one day and appreciate the person your child has become.

The Narrow Path

Scripture reading: Mark 11:22-24

Spiritual Guides

A Few Suggestions for Me as a Mother: Keep communication open at all times. Permit person-to-person phone calls. Let them know that they are loved and welcome at home. Permit the children to disagree with me, provided they do it respectfully. (And I find occasionally they are right and I am wrong.) Make a clear distinction between moral and nonmoral issues. Encourage. (Ruth Bell Graham, *Prodigals and Those Who Love Them*)

Light on the Path

Without warning, a furious storm came up on the lake, so that the waves swept over the boat. But Jesus was sleeping. The disciples went and woke him, saying, "Lord, save us! We're going to drown!"

He replied, "You of little faith, why are you so afraid?" Then he got up and rebuked the winds and the waves, and it was completely calm. (Matthew 8:24-26)

1. The preteen and teenage stages can sometimes be stormy. What things do you fear about this age with your children? Practice confession by making a list of your fears before God. Practice the discipline of study by looking up passages related to your fears.

2. Prayerfully make a game plan for how you will react to certain inevitable milestones in your child's maturing process. For example, how do you plan to tell him about sex?

3. Think of one thing you can do today to encourage your child.

Your Traveling Companion

Meditate on this chapter's Scripture reading: "Therefore I tell you, whatever you ask for in prayer, believe that you have received it, and it will be yours" (Mark 11:24). Ask God, *Keep a hedge around my child. Draw him into your Holy Presence.*

Chapter Nine

Reaping a Harvest of Righteousness

"Well, spring has definitely arrived!" Joshua flopped on my bed, a scowl on his face.

I continued to put away clean laundry. "What's the matter?" I asked.

"The first warm day, and most of the girls had hardly any clothes on!" he sighed.

I laughed at my fifteen-year-old's observation of "spring fever." Patting him on the back, I said, "So it was a kind of a bad day, huh?"

"Bad? Mom, I don't want to lust after those girls! But when they don't have any clothes on, what *am* I supposed to do?"

"I think you know the answer to that question," I responded. "You're doing it right now by confessing your struggles." I gave Joshua a hug and told him how pleased I was that he didn't try to face these battles on his own. "You know that James tells us when we confess our sins we are healed. You obeyed His Word so God will help you overcome this."

The years of encouraging our children to practice the spiritual disciplines were starting to bear fruit. The times Tim and I had wanted to give up, but persevered at guiding our boys, now all seemed worth it.

But we knew the hard work had just begun. It certainly wasn't time to cruise. Joshua still had several more "springs" ahead and his younger brother was right behind him. Yet, hearing my son's confession that afternoon reassured me that the narrow path we had chosen to walk as a family was headed in the right direction—into the presence of God.

Have you ever wondered why so many kids end up falling away from the church? I got a firsthand look at this phenomena when Joshua and Josiah were part of their marching band. In order to be involved with my sons' lives, I volunteered to be the "uniform mom." Knowing the pants and shoe sizes of 150 kids put me in a very intimate position. As I grew closer to many of the students, they confided in and trusted in me. At times Joshua resented Mom being at school so much, but after graduation, he admitted that he knew it was "his salvation."

From my view as "uniform mom" I saw many teenagers, even those raised in the church or with high moral standards, experimenting with alcohol, drugs and sex. I'm certain that there were many causes for their rebellion and they were definitely making their own choices. Yet why do so many of these kids come out of religion and want no part of it? I believe it's because they want nothing to do with the outward motivations of fear and guilt that much of religion places on our children. Since the spiritual disciplines are not often taught, encouraged or practiced, many teenagers lack an inward relationship with God to sustain them through these turbulent years.

As I stated in an earlier chapter, there are no guarantees. There are a lot of good parents doing all the right things. Whenever I hear of people all but lynching the parents of teens who have turned to crime, I want to speak up in their defense. I realize parents should have some sort of clue when something goes wrong with their children. But how many of us have thought, *My child would never do that*? After a recent shooting at a local high school, a friend confessed that she hoped that the teens involved had bad parents. She didn't particularly want to hear that the parents were abusive, just neglectful. It would reassure her that her own kids might not turn sour.

Having experienced the hurt caused by a deceitful son, I know the times parents of troubled kids may have called their son's work to check on him, only to realize later that his adult supervisor lied for him. Or how often a mother might have driven by her daughter's friend's house to make sure her car is there, not realizing that she had sneaked away with someone else? No matter how many times parents search a room or challenge a questionable story, a heart bent on evil will go its own way. However, a child with a soft heart toward God will receive the training of the spiritual disciplines.

When children reach the teen years, they desire to develop their own convictions. The beliefs of their parents seem to lack appeal and therefore often teens experiment to find their own. Satan knows this all too well. During Joshua's junior year in high school he enrolled in a social studies class that, according to description, would explore the different religions of the world. In reality, the teacher had a definite agenda—to poison the hearts and minds of her students against Christianity. At the beginning of the semester the teacher announced that they would all go "against their parents' belief systems." She then proceeded to teach that God is a woman and that Western religion (Christianity) is to blame for all social calamities, such as child abuse, racism, rape and much more.

Joshua watched as kids who professed to be Christians and were active in their churches participated in a mixture of Buddhism, Hinduism, Taoism and other ancient religions. Although the class description listed Christianity and Judaism, the teacher refused to address these belief systems until Joshua pressured her to do so. Our son shared the truth of Christ through his writings, class discussions and presentations and by refusing to participate in Eastern meditation practices. When the teacher strongly suggested that Joshua drop the class, he declined in hopes of reaching the hearts of his classmates or perhaps even the teacher.

On the final day of the semester, the students were given time to share the things they learned from the class. Many students remarked at Joshua's boldness, even though they didn't agree with him. Several said that they would always remember his words before the class. Joshua came home that day and plopped on my bed again. This time his eyes filled with tears because so many of the students had renounced their faith in Christ to follow this teacher.

This experience reinforced Tim's and my belief in the importance of teaching the spiritual disciplines to our children from the start of their lives. When the time came for Joshua to stand up for his convictions, he sensed the presence of God with him. He had learned the difference between Eastern meditation and meditating on God's Word. He studied the Scriptures diligently in order to counteract the false teachings thrown at him every day. When asked in which of the Hindu realms he felt his soul abided, Joshua could give an answer. He told his classmates that he lived in the "reality of the truth of Christ" and not in any realm, especially the Hell Realm. He shared in front of the classroom that when he sinned he confessed it and because Christ had overcome hell, he could be forgiven and healed. Those types of beliefs and convictions could not have been taught overnight to our son. They came from a lifetime of training.

Just as when they were younger, we try not to give our teens more than they can handle. As they move toward independence, the amount of freedom and decision-making must match the level of a child's maturity. One of our temporary custody daughters was enrolled in the same world religion class as Joshua. After the first month, it was obvious that the teacher's poison had affected her. She began to shut us out and said that the teacher taught that everyone had a "secret place within them," where parents had no right to invade. Needless to say we pulled her from the class while Joshua continued.

Although teenagers try to "spread their wings" and test their philosophies, they like to know that their parents are in the background. (Don't believe your teenager when he tells you to stay out of his life.) We allowed Joshua to fight this battle, but under our watchful eyes. Tim gathered information and advice on what our legal rights were in this situation. We both helped Joshua when he had questions about the philosophies taught. We didn't scold or make judgments when our son wrestled with rebellion or questioned our beliefs because of the influence of the class. My husband and I discussed, guided and prayed with Joshua through this time.

Parents just starting to practice the spiritual disciplines in their own lives may feel it's too late for their children, but it's not. It's time to "Wake up, O sleeper, rise from the dead, and Christ will shine on you" (Ephesians 5:14). No matter the ages of your children, prayerfully ask God how to begin practicing the disciplines.

This book mainly deals with how to instill the disciplines in little ones, because of God's commands. But many of us didn't come to know God until adulthood. Some of you may have raised your kids in front of the television or by very permissive standards. It's never too late to bring discipline into our lives. You will have to go back to the basics, even trying some of the suggestions for younger kids listed in this book. It may take longer and require more work, but if you feel that God's discipline is worth it in your life, then it is for your children as well.

And you have forgotten that word of encouragement that addresses you as sons:

"My son, do not make light of the Lord's discipline,
    and do not lose heart when he rebukes you,
because the Lord disciplines those he loves,
    and he punishes everyone he accepts as a son."

Endure hardship as discipline; God is treating you as sons. For what son is not disciplined by his father? If you are not disciplined (and everyone undergoes discipline), then you are illegitimate children and not true sons. Moreover, we have all had human fathers who disciplined us and we respected them for it. How much more should we submit to the Father of our spirits and live! Our fathers disciplined us for a little while as they thought best; but God disciplines us for our good, that we may share in his holiness. *No discipline*

seems pleasant at the time, but painful. Later on, however, it
produces a harvest of righteousness and peace for those who
have been trained by it.

Therefore, strengthen your feeble arms and weak knees.
(Hebrews 12:5-12, italics added)

A careful look at this passage tells us the kind of parents we need to be with our children. First of all discipline is a sign of love. If we do not discipline our children, we are treating them as illegitimate. I believe this also applies to the spiritual disciplines as well as the disciplines that control behavior. Remember that the inward disciplines are what guide the outward behavior. Use the spiritual disciplines in your own life to guide you in your children's lives. Doing so will produce a harvest of righteousness for anyone who allows discipline to train him or her.

All through this book, I've said that parents must honestly evaluate their kids' hearts and motives. This is probably even more important when they reach the teen years. If we don't see our children clearly, then we'll miss opportunities for God's discipline to work. Maybe you have a teenager who doesn't want anything to do with God or religion. Or perhaps your teen wants God, but is not used to discipline. Honestly evaluating your kids can sometimes be scary. When Josiah began to show some signs of rebellion that were similar to our oldest child, I prayed, *Oh God, not again.* Remember God's words to Joshua, "Be strong and courageous. Do not be terrified; do not be discouraged, for the LORD your God will be with you wherever you go" (Joshua 1:9).

As our society lowers its standards, parents need to raise the values by which we expect our children to live. Parents must teach their children the following passage: "Therefore come out from them and be separate, says the Lord. Touch no unclean thing, and I will receive you" (2 Corinthians 6:17). Take a good look at your children. How have you compromised in their dress, hairstyles, language, bedroom posters or activities, thinking, "It's just a phase?" I cannot tell you the times I have mentioned that a certain family is Christian, only to have my children inform me that the sons and daughters of those families don't act or dress any differently. They use foul language, break curfew, drink, smoke and lie to their parents. And I am certain that people thought the same about our family as they watched our oldest son's life.

We cannot believe that just because our children sit in our pews and attend youth groups that they are OK. Parents must see their children clearly and fight against the standards of the world. We have to pick our battles wisely and about the smallest of issues—early bedtimes, stricter dress standards, fewer video games, friends they hang with—before we lose total control of our children. As parents, we need to stop and admit the "little" things we let slip by us. Practicing the spiritual disciplines gives us guidelines for our standards and values.

Most teenagers will try to test their parents' standards. Joshua was no exception. He wanted to dress like everyone at school—shirt opened with a T-shirt exposed, his hat on backward. We weren't very rigid with how we approached our son on the issue. A little humor and understanding kept the lines of communication open between us. He knew the standards we desired so that he might glorify the Lord with his dress. For instance, we would usually remain silent when we noticed his shirt opened. Later, however, when he would ask permission to do something, such as borrow the car, we might make a light-hearted joke about his attire: "Well, I don't know. Anyone who can't dress himself correctly, maybe can't drive a car." Joshua would laugh and quickly button his shirt. Eventually, our son began to realize that his witness to classmates and teachers was more effective if he dressed neater.

Realize that the phases teenagers go through are normal and somewhat predictable. But their behavior still has to be dealt with or it will remain. I often think of the teen years as the "terrible twos" all over again. Toddlers desire independence but really have no idea how to handle freedom. So when boundaries are set to protect them, two-year-olds throw tantrums and demand their way. If allowed to continue in this behavior, they become spoiled and rebellious. The same thing is true with teenagers. They cry for freedom and fewer rules, but teens have no idea how to use their independence responsibly.

Ask other parents who have gone through the teenage stage and have lived to talk about it. Find out the behaviors that are common to the different ages. For instance, after the Jell-O years pass, the "I Know It Alls" begin. Your child suddenly becomes an expert on everything. Decide which issues are really worth arguing about and which ones you can let go. Having had several temporary custody daughters, I now realize that fifteen-year-old girls usually go through an "I hate Mom" stage and try to wrap Daddy around their little finger. Again, you have to pick your battles prayerfully and not take your child's behavior personally.

If we don't set boundaries in our teenagers' lives, they can get hurt or go down undesirable paths. When you do tell them no, they revert to the "terrible twos" and kick and scream. Parents must set boundaries regardless of how their children respond if they hope to see them grow into responsible, considerate adults. Here are some ways that you can use the spiritual disciplines to set boundaries for teens:

Prayer

- ♥ If your child professes that he wants to follow God, then communication with the Father is vital. But forcing a child to pray will only instill guilt and encourage outward motivation. Encourage, demonstrate, prod and suggest, but never force a child to pray.

- ♥ Pray often with your child. Don't worry if he seems embarrassed to pray with you.

- ♥ Purchase notebooks for prayer journaling. Don't be concerned if he balks at using a journal. My boys didn't like to journal for years; now they keep better journals than me.

- ♥ Encourage your child to write a prayer for someone they are not getting along with, or a difficult situation at school or home.

💜 Help your child establish a regular time of prayer. Since we had quiet times all their lives, our sons naturally start their day with prayer. Like most seniors, Joshua's last year of high school was full and busy. As drum major his responsibilities and time constraints increased. He would sleep in every morning and get up just in time to get himself dressed and to school by the 7:15 bell. At first I worried about his lack of morning prayer, but very gently reminded him that he must not forget to pray. A little encouragement goes a long way. Joshua started coming home during his off period in the morning to spend time in the Word and prayer.

💜 Don't hesitate to pray, even if your teenager refuses to pray with you. Set the example of keeping up the disciplines in your own life.

Worship

💜 Remember that worship is our opportunity to give back to God. Teach your teenager that there are many ways to show God that we love and adore Him. Through obedience, song, poetry and prayer we can worship God. But remember these are not to be worshiped themselves. Brother Lawrence said, "Abandon any other concerns, including any special devotions you've undertaken simply as a means to an end. *God* is our end."[1]

💜 Continue to have times of family worship. Buy CDs of praise music or classic hymns, including the ones your teens want. Play music in the car and around the house.

💜 Musically inclined teenagers can be encouraged to use their talents in public or private worship. Joshua uses his guitar to praise God often during his morning or evening prayer times.

💜 If your teen announces that he no longer wants to attend church, you must prayerfully seek God's wisdom. Ask Him to help you determine how deep the rebellion lies in your child. Many teenagers balk at going to church, but once they attend they find it enjoyable. It will take wisdom from the Lord to know how far to push your teen. You can claim the promise of Colossians 1:28: "We proclaim him, admonishing and teaching everyone with *all wisdom*, so that we may present everyone perfect in Christ" (italics added).

♥ Encourage your children to have a holy expectation that they will feel God's presence during worship. Our church family meets on Sunday afternoons at 1:30, rather than in the morning, so that we are not rushed but prepared to worship. When families fight on the way to church and come into worship frazzled, they have anything but an expectation of God.

♥ Continue to teach your children to look for ways to praise God and to show Him thankfulness. Encourage them to have "Thanksgiving Moments," stopping to thank God for His blessings.

Study

♥ We all want our kids to make good judgments. Teaching them the Word of God guides our children to make sound choices. "Teach me knowledge and good judgment, for I believe in your commands" (Psalm 119:66).

♥ Provide teenagers with updated versions of classic spiritual writers such as Brother Lawrence and Thomas à Kempis. Joshua collects books by his favorite author, Andrew Murray. When the kids were younger, they enjoyed a video production of John Bunyan's *Pilgrim's Progress* and as teens they wanted to read this classic story of Pilgrim's journey to heaven.

♥ Since Joshua had learning disabilities, we obtained books on tape for many of his school books as well as for classic books. The boys like to listen to Scripture tapes as they fall asleep or drive.

Meditation

♥ Your teenager might balk at reading the Bible if he is rebelling against your beliefs. Tacking up a passage on the fridge or bulletin board will put God's Word in his mind and hopefully his heart. A friend has cross-stitched several Scripture references for me that are scattered throughout our home.

♥ Your teenager is going to meditate on something—a teen magazine, a favorite television program, what to wear tomorrow. Encourage your child to meditate on the Word by pointing him to particular passages that seem to apply to his life.

♥ Screen your teen's activities, computer games, TV and movies. As I mentioned before, Tim and I screened many a movie before our children viewed them, especially after our children were in high school.

♥ Taking a stand not to date helped our teens have pure hearts and minds and a determination to "take captive every thought to make it obedient to Christ" (2 Corinthians 10:5).

Solitude

♥ It's not too hard to get teenagers to spend time alone. They tend to hide in their "caves" with their music blaring. Screen the music they like to listen to underneath their headphones and provide music that will point them toward the Lord.

♥ Joshua hated the fact that all through high school we expected him to climb into bed at a decent hour, especially since most of his friends apparently had no "regular bedtime." In reality, he seldom was in bed at the time we set, but much earlier than if we hadn't set any bedtime. Now on his own, he expresses gratitude for this discipline. He uses this time of solitude to quiet his soul before the Lord, and says with the Psalmist, "On my bed I remember you; I think of you through the watches of the night" (Psalm 63:6).

❤ Your teenager may practice solitude not to get close to God but as a means of withdrawing, because he is shy. Encourage a shy teen to socialize by helping him to become involved in church fellowship. The Apostle Paul tells us to "encourage the timid, help the weak, be patient with everyone" (1 Thessalonians 5:14).

❤ Invite your teen to find his own place of solitude. In our household this sometimes was difficult. But we always tried to provide and encouraged the kids to find a place where they could be still with God—even if that meant the bathroom!

❤ When God seems to be stripping away the self and sin in your child's life, he will need times of solitude to reflect. If he doesn't want to talk, honor his silence. Pray for his heart to feel God's prodding if confession is needed. Make sure he understands that you are waiting to listen when he is ready.

Fasting

❤ At this stage our children made the decision whether God was calling them into fasting. Then they would ask our permission to fast so they could draw nearer to the Lord.

❤ Make sure that fasting is called by God and focused on Him. Many teenagers deal with appearance issues and get caught up in fad diets.

❤ If your teenager is having a particularly hard time overcoming a sin, fast on his behalf. Petition God to give your child victory over his struggles.

Confession

❤ Always keep an open line of communication with your teenager. Let him know that there is nothing he could do that

God would not forgive him for, and tell him that you would also forgive him.

💛 When you sense that your child may have done something wrong or as he confesses, reason with him to find out his motives and issues. Help him to see the *why* of his actions. Show him the way to repentance.

💛 Set the example of confession. When your child was younger, you might have been able to get by with "little" sins in your own life, but teenagers resent hypocrisy.

💛 We must expect our children to be truthful in their motives, speech and actions if we desire for them to enter into the presence of He who is Truth. "Surely you desire truth in the inner parts; you teach me wisdom in the inmost place" (Psalm 51:6).

Guidance

💛 Teach your teenager to seek God's will in all things. Don't give him answers too quickly. Let him wrestle for solutions with the Lord. This becomes more important the older he gets, since you will not always be around to make decisions for him.

💛 Point him toward Scripture to find out what Jesus might do in a particular situation. Nudge your child to have the same mind as Christ when He said, "I do nothing on my own but speak just what the Father has taught me" (John 8:28).

💛 Teenagers need spiritual directors in their lives. If your child doesn't respond to you in this role, then help him seek someone else that you can trust to guide your child in the same way you would. Watch carefully that this relationship points him closer to God and not just that person.

Service

♥ Teach your child to be dependent on the Lord when serving, since Jesus warned his disciples, "apart from me you can do nothing" (John 15:5).

♥ Don't allow your child to get caught up in *doing* without making sure he is *being* in the presence of the Lord. If you sense this happening, pull him aside from service for a time to seek God's will.

♥ Continue to find ways for your child to serve in the community. Since I spent a lot of time at the high school, I discovered ways to encourage my boys to serve teachers, school secretaries and classmates.

♥ We taught the kids when they were little that we served one another because we were a family that loved. Continue to encourage this attitude with your teenager. Discuss which chores he thinks would be the best ways for him to serve the family.

Submission

♥ Determine what boundaries you will set in areas such as curfews, homework, bedtime, eating habits, friends and activities, dating and literally every aspect of your child's life. What consequences will you have for stepping out of those boundaries?

♥ Expect your child to submit without grumbling but with joy. Your rules are for his best and he should understand that, but don't expect him to admit it. We told our boys this passage applied to parents as well as church leaders: "Obey your leaders and submit to their authority. They keep watch over you as men who must give an account. Obey them so that their work will be a joy, not a burden, for that would be of no advantage to you" (Hebrews 13:17).

❤ If others in the home have not maintained a submissive attitude, you will have a hard time getting your teenager to submit. For instance, if Mom has obviously manipulated Dad into doing what she wants, and he has allowed it, his daughter will figure she can manipulate him, too.

❤ Have a long-term goal for your rules. What do you hope to accomplish in your child by expecting submission on a particular issue? For instance, our dress code rules of no backward hats or open shirts was so that our sons would glorify God and not look like part of the "hood."

❤ Don't lay down so many rules that you exasperate your child. This takes a lot of prayer and self-denial on the part of the parent. Ask God to show you how to reason and prod your teen to the cross and a point of brokenness, but not exasperation. "Fathers, do not exasperate your children; instead, bring them up in the training and instruction of the Lord" (Ephesians 6:4).

Simplicity

❤ Purge your possessions often and have your children do the same.

❤ Pray with your child for the Holy Spirit's guidance on what might make his life simpler. Does he need more storage space or does he need to clean out? Does he need more time to do homework? Does he have too many outside activities? Compare his time spent in the Word to his other commitments.

❤ I've discovered the more contemplative my prayer life becomes the more simplistic my life. This has been true in my children's lives as well. The closer they draw into God's presence the more content they have become.

Celebration

💜 Try not to overly celebrate outward achievements. Focus on the inner growth and express thankfulness for submission, confession and disciplined lives.

💜 Sometimes parents tend to stop attending school functions once their child reaches high school. Continue to participate and celebrate with your child his accomplishments. But at the same time, keep the cross before him, reminding him that all good things come from God.

💜 Remember that obedience leads to joy. The more you expect your teenager to obey, the happier your household becomes.

💜 Strive to have a mind-set of rejoicing always in the Lord. Laughter is contagious. If we are happy, our children will be too.

So, why do so many teenagers fall away from the church? I think the following passage sums it up:

> But mark this: There will be terrible times in the last days. People will be lovers of themselves, lovers of money, boastful, proud, abusive, disobedient to their parents, ungrateful, unholy, without love, unforgiving, slanderous, without self-control, brutal, not lovers of the good, treacherous, rash, conceited, lovers of pleasure rather than lovers of God—having a form of godliness but denying its power. Have nothing to do with them. (2 Timothy 3:1-5)

Raising our standards by teaching our children to have spiritual discipline in their lives gives them the motivation to have nothing to do with "lovers of pleasure rather than lovers of God."

Spring rolled around again and Joshua found himself again dealing with the girls. We could sense his struggle because he was silent and distant for several days. Joshua came into my bedroom one night right before I fell asleep. This time he knelt beside my bed. With tears he said, "Mom, I'm sorry. I've been dealing with rebellion toward you and Dad." Joshua went on to confess how he felt the pull toward girls again and how his rebellion was a way to cover up his own sin. I forgave him and we prayed. He asked God to discipline his heart so that he would stop dealing with lust. And you know what? The next spring, he rejoiced in knowing that God had answered his prayer.

The Narrow Path

Scripture reading: 1 John 4:16

Spiritual Guides

That God cares enough about us to regulate the details of our lives is the strongest proof of love He could give; and that He should condescend to tell us all about it, and to let us know just how to live and walk so as perfectly to please Him seems almost too good to be true. We never care about the little details of people's lives unless we love them. . . . God's law, therefore, is only another name for God's love. (Hannah Whitall Smith, *The Christian's Secret of a Happy Life*)

Light on the Path

Love is patient, love is kind. It does not envy, it does not boast, it is not proud. It is not rude, it is not self-seeking, it is not easily angered, it keeps no record of wrongs. Love does not delight in evil but rejoices with the truth. It always protects, always trusts, always hopes, always perseveres.

Love never fails. (1 Corinthians 13:4-8)

1. Meditate on the above passage. What aspects of love do you have a hard time expressing to your children?

2. What things do you see in your child that make it hard to "rejoice in the truth?" Do any of these mirror aspects of your own personality?

3. Do you find it difficult to accept God's law as love? How is it hard to "lay down the law" in your child's life?

Your Traveling Companion

Ask God to place each attribute of First Corinthians 13 love in your heart. Ask, *Please strip away my self-seeking love for Your perfect love.*

Chapter Ten

GENERATION TO GENERATION

A lways remember to love Jesus with all your heart. . . . It's your turn," Grandpa Ray would encourage me as we played Chinese checkers. My great-grandfather died when I was small, but his words lived on in my heart. His wife, Grandma Missy, bowed on her knees every night in their living room where we could join her for prayer and Bible reading if we wanted. Grandpa Ray's love for the Lord carried on with his daughter—my Granny.

I've been told that I was only two days old the first time I ever entered the church. As I grew, my mother tried to keep me quiet during services by providing crayons and paper. Until one Sunday when I shook the box to unstick a crayon and twenty-three of its companions went flying in the air, landing on a sleeping man in the pew in front of us. Needless to say, the crayons never attended church again. But they were replaced with a child's devotional that became one of my dearest treasures.

Then came the day when I could be trusted enough to sit still in the front pew—a place of honor for "good little children." When my younger brother reached this milestone, he always fell asleep and snored loudly. Not me. I didn't want to miss anything our beloved minister had to say. As a child, church was my home, my social circle, my life. Granny made certain that what we learned at church we lived at home. She won my father over for the Lord and soon our family life became centered around Him.

Then something happened. We moved to a different town and a different church, where my father was quickly put in leadership. My mother grew ill and things slowly began to change. God no longer seemed to be the central focus of our lives. Oh, we spoke His name often and always prayed before meals. But our morning and evening family devotions were replaced with *The Today Show* and *Gilligan's Island*. The strict rules of "no or very little television" were replaced with, "Is your homework done? OK, you can watch." Jesus didn't leave our home overnight. It was a slow progression. In fact, it was so slow and quiet that we didn't detect His departure.

My family never stopped going to church—twice on Sunday and every Wednesday night. Our church didn't believe in ordained ministers so Daddy preached every fourth Sunday. At nine I knew I wanted to follow my grandfather's advice and "love Jesus with all my heart." So I asked to be baptized. Now that I look back, maybe I was a little too young. But it was the one focal point in my life that I always held on to. Soon my brother and sister followed—mainly so our father could qualify for eldership. We continued to go to church—twice on Sunday and every Wednesday night.

When I reached my teen years, it became acutely evident, to me at least, that Jesus wasn't a member of our church. I shuddered during a chorus of "one will be taken and other left behind." I feared that perhaps God had abandoned me along with everyone else sitting in the pews. By this time the church had split at least three times and my father was preaching every Sunday, as well as leading the singing. My mother stopped attending completely, due to her illness, and I slipped into her position of the elder/preacher's wife. Once at summer camp, I asked the pastor from our original church what could be done about the problems in our church. His advice, "Go home and lay down your life for those people."

And oh, how I tried to do just that! I worked harder at loving the woman who started most of the fighting and gossip. I taught Sunday school with more zeal. I read my Bible and journaled my prayers every day. I tried to rally what was left of the youth. But Jesus just didn't seem to want to return to my little rural church.

At home Mom grew more ill and demanded more attention. I hid myself in community service work and helping disabled children. I tried so hard to keep my position in the front pew, yet rebellion grew in my heart. Finally, I became so disillusioned that I began to search for satisfaction apart from God and His Word. So on Saturday nights I partied with my friends and the next morning taught Sunday school. My life was a mess. I begged God, *Don't let Grandpa Ray see what I am doing.* Somehow I sensed that he stood with the "cloud of witnesses" praying that I would throw off the sin that entangled my life (Hebrews 12:1).

Fortunately God allowed me to hit my brick wall after graduating from high school and before completely destroying myself. As I shared previously, motherhood stopped my downward spiral. The first couple of years were tough for Tim and me, but we kept longing to enter the presence of God. The bitterness and resentment toward my mother's illness melted away when the Lord impressed on my heart the truth of Acts 17:26—that God had determined the circumstances I grew up in. Years later, when I discovered that her illness was imaginary and not physical, I felt no regret. I knew exactly why I had been placed in her family, and could love her and pray for her like never before. I truly believe that memories of playing Chinese checkers and bouncing on Granny's knee kept my heart pointed toward God during my rebellious years. God's presence remained with me, even though I shut Him out.

After my own children were born, I wanted their relationship with God not to be based on performance. Tim has always prayed that his sons would surpass him in holiness and righteousness. God has more than answered his prayers through our two youngest sons. And our hope remains steadfast for their older brother.

But it did not come without sacrifice and hard work. We were often misunderstood, especially by family members, for our resolve "to know nothing . . . except Jesus Christ and him crucified" (1 Corinthians 2:2). Our stand to screen their television viewing and our views on dating aroused exaggerated accusations of being too strict on our sons. But like Paul, we taught our children how to "use the things of the world, as if not engrossed in them" (7:31). We even purchased copies of old television sitcoms (including *Gilligan's Island*), yet we taught them how to discern right from wrong in those programs.

Our boys have grown up with the usual scrapes and bruises, struggles and rebellion, desires and decisions that all children experience. Tim and I understood the danger of becoming "too righteous," as Ecclesiastes says: "Do not be overrighteous, neither be overwise—why destroy yourself?" (7:16). So we allowed our children to discover how to live in this world without becoming caught up in it. We chose to "walk along the way" with them, guiding and helping them to have spiritually disciplined lives.

Though in this book I have suggested many things for you to do with your own children "along the way," one thing is sure: your children will not earn a position in the front pew by self-effort. The kind of life depicted in the pages of this book is one of continual self-denial as His Spirit leads. We have hope that our children will see God, "if by the Spirit you put to death the misdeeds of the body" (Romans 8:13). Something new happens every day in our children's lives. They learn new skills. They battle with different temptations. We must be willing to allow God to prune us and strip away all of self so we can help the Gardener do His work in their lives.

> I am the true vine, and my Father is the gardener. He cuts
> off every branch in me that bears no fruit, while every branch
> that does bear fruit he prunes so that it will be even more
> fruitful. You are already clean because of the word I have

spoken to you. Remain in me, and I will remain in you. No
branch can bear fruit by itself; it must remain in the vine.
Neither can you bear fruit unless you remain in me.

I am the vine; you are the branches. If a man remains in me
and I in him, he will bear much fruit; apart from me you can
do nothing. (John 15:1-5)

Stripping our lives of what feels comfortable and familiar is a painful process that only the cross can work. It is the kind of pain that Jesus
felt when He sweat drops of blood praying, "Your will be done." Unfortunately, we often do not even realize that we need stripping. Like
the Israelites who became comfortable in their Babylonian captivity,
we become clueless of our sin. Worse yet, we cause our children to become complacent along with us. As Tim wrote in his book, *The Whisper Revival: Our Only Option*:

> People in captivity drag their children with them. . . . Since
> the parents raised them in captivity, claiming that the Lord
> blessed them, their children never experience the sweetness
> of true fellowship with the Lord and never see the resur-
> rected life in their parents. They think that the unrighteous
> deeds and self-justifications of their parents constitute the
> Christian walk. They never see their parents surrender every-
> thing to God, but live the Christian life on their own terms.[1]

Surrendering to God's will in our lives sometimes can be easier than
allowing His will to be done in our children. It's hard to watch as they
suffer and struggle. Shortly before Josiah's sinus infection incident,
Tim and I had asked God to strip away anything that kept our son from
loving Him with all his heart. Little did we know God would put Josiah
to the test in such a dramatic way and at the same time strip our own
hearts again.

In order to break our wills and teach us to accept His breaking in our
children's hearts, He has to bring us to the foot of the cross. There He

"shows us what real brokenness is," Roy Hession says. "We see those wounded hands and feet, that face of love crowned with thorns, and we see the complete brokenness of the One who said, 'Not my will, but Thine.' "[2] When we see the love God had for us to lay down His own Son, we want our own sons and daughters to be broken by His love.

The way we respond to God's discipline in our lives will set the pattern for our children. Our response to our oldest son's denial of God strengthened our two youngest to stand firm for the Lord. I went through a time of mourning, but God impressed on my heart that I had other children to raise for Him. I could wallow in self-pity or allow the Gardener to strip my branches. Surrendering to His pruning shears allowed me to confess my mistakes and press on. There would be many more times of God breaking my heart yet to come and it would be a constant choice of allowing His discipline to work. Each time God breaks me, however, it also brings my children just a little closer to His will. I no longer want to make them conform to my will.

When we stand at the foot of the cross we realize that the brokenness in our lives is God's work, not ours. We realize our unworthiness and how much His grace is a gift. His grace frees us from the path of sin and spurs us on to spiritually disciplined lives. One of the most freeing passages in my life, and one I've tried to pass on to my children, is Titus 2:11-13:

> For the grace of God that brings salvation has appeared to all men. It teaches us to say "No" to ungodliness and worldly passions, and to live self-controlled, upright and godly lives in this present age, while we wait for the blessed hope—the glorious appearing of our great God and Savior, Jesus Christ.

God's grace is more than a quick prayer of salvation and a pat on the head. It is powerful and life-changing. Grace urges me to want to practice the spiritual disciplines in order to say "No" to the temptations of this world. God's grace in my life causes me to show grace to my children—a grace that expects them to change and to live godly lives, and gives them power to do so through the cross.

God's grace brings me back to the foot of the cross. I look up and see the Son of God who "being found in appearance as a man, he humbled himself and became obedient to death—even death on a cross!" (Philippians 2:8). Jesus' humility provokes me to humble myself and feel my sense of nothingness.

Humility is where I can feel God's presence. It humbles me to realize that by His grace God placed me in Grandpa Ray's family so I would someday cry out to Him. Humbling myself before God shows me that I cannot do anything in this book except by His Spirit. No matter how hard I try to enforce the spiritual disciplines in my life or the lives of my children, it is worthless if done without humility. As Jesus taught His disciples, "The Spirit gives life; the flesh counts for nothing. The words I have spoken to you are spirit and they are life" (John 6:63).

Tim often reminds our family how much we must depend on the Holy Spirit by asking, "How much is 100 x 0?" When the kids first learned their multiplication tables they thought this was a silly question. "Oh Dad, it's *zero*, of course!" they would chime. He would explain to them that anything they did outside of God's will and power—no matter how right it seemed—would equal a big, fat zero. No matter how hard we try to pray, confess, serve or do any of the other disciplines, if we do it in our own power it amounts to nothing.

I think it's important to note the response of some disciples to Jesus' words. They had been following Him and trying to obey everything He taught. But when it came time to surrender all and allow the Spirit to control their lives, they turned back. "He went on to say, 'This is why I told you that no one can come to me unless the Father has enabled him.' From this time many of his disciples turned back and no longer followed him" (6:65-66).

The passage says that many of those following Jesus no longer followed Him. As you strive to teach your children to surrender all and allow the Spirit to work the disciplines in their lives, they may choose not to follow. Like many of the disciples, one or all your children may say,

"This is a hard teaching. Who can accept it?" (6:60). The way of self-denial is a hard road. But if we hope to lead our children, we parents must have the same attitude as Peter when Jesus asked the chosen Twelve if they wanted to leave too: "Lord, to whom shall we go? You have the words of eternal life" (6:68).

Practicing the spiritual disciplines in our family helped our children enter God's presence and hear the "words of eternal life." Where should we go, but toward the path of spiritual discipline? God gave His children the freedom of choice. Although some may choose not to follow, our hope lies in continuing with the disciplines. "Discipline your son, for in that there is hope; do not be a willing party to his death" (Proverbs 19:18).

I may never have grandchildren of my own with whom I pass on God's treasure of the spiritual disciplines. But I have tasted and seen that the Lord is good (Psalm 34:8). He has given me many opportunities through ministry, writing and speaking to teach young parents how to teach their children the spiritual disciplines. God has blessed me with many spiritual grandsons and granddaughters who call me "Granny Carla" and sit on my lap singing, "Roamie, Roamie." But more importantly, they get excited when they hear the words "quiet time," because they know it's time to learn about Jesus. It's time to enter the presence of God.

As this book draws to a close, it is my hope and prayer that you have been inspired to pick up your cross. I pray that the suggestions I have listed will light the path of spiritual discipline in your life, that you will prayerfully consider how God would have you live out these things by the power of His Spirit. My prayer is that we will all learn to love God with all our heart, soul, mind and strength as we "walk along the way," and that we will teach our children that "His mercy extends to those who fear him, from generation to generation" (Luke 1:50).

Appendix A

~ ^ ~ ^ ~ ^ ~ ^ ~ ^ ~ ^ ~ ^ ~ ^ ~ ^ ~

RECOMMENDED READING

I've divided the recommended reading list into categories to help parents seek resources for their particular needs. This list is by no means comprehensive. It will, however, give you a start in the right direction as you walk along the way.

Personal Spiritual Encouragement for Parents

The following list of books are "must reads" for any Christian who hopes to pursue the spiritual disciplines in his or her life.

Brother Lawrence. *The Practice of the Presence of God*. New Kensington, PA: Whitaker House, 1982.

Foster, Richard. *Celebration of Discipline*. Revised edition. San Francisco: Harper and Row, 1988. *(Editor's Note: We strongly suggest the use of the revised edition, in which wording has been changed to improve accuracy and understanding.)*

Murray, Andrew. *Humility*. New Kensington, PA: Whitaker House, 1982 edition.

Johnson, Jan. *Enjoying the Presence of God*. Colorado Springs, CO: NavPress, 1996.

Johnson, Jan. *When the Soul Listens*. Colorado Springs, CO: NavPress, 1999.

Smith, Hannah Whitall. *The Christian's Secret of a Happy Life*. Old Tappan, NJ: Revell/Spire, 1966.

Tozer, A.W. *The Pursuit of God*. Camp Hill, PA: Christian Publications, Inc., 1993.

Tozer, A.W. *The Root of the Righteous*. Camp Hill, PA: Christian Publications, Inc., 1993.

Williams, Timothy. *The Essential Piece*. Enumclaw, WA: WinePress, 2000.

Parenting Books

Cloud, Dr. Henry and Dr. John Townsend. *Raising Great Kids*. Grand Rapids, MI: Zondervan, 1999.

Graham, Ruth Bell. *Prodigals and Those Who Love Them*. Colorado Springs: Focus on the Family, 1991.

Ketterman, Dr. Grace. *Parenting the Difficult Child*. Nashville: Thomas Nelson, 1994.

Sears, Dr. William. *Parenting and Child Care*. Revised edition. Nashville: Thomas Nelson, 1993.

Wilson, Wayne. *Worldly Amusements*. Enumclaw, WA: WinePress, 1999.

Children's Devotional Material

There are dozens of devotionals for all ages on the market. These are just a few of my favorites.

Barclift, Stephen. *The Beginner's Devotional*. Sisters, OR: Questar, 1991.

The Children's Discovery Bible. Colorado Springs: Chariot Victor, 1996.

Elkins, Stephen. *The Words & Song Bible* (with CDs or Cassettes). Nashville: Broadman and Holman, 1999.

Pershetti, Jackie. *Dangerous Devotions* (Series: Old and New Testaments). Colorado Springs: Chariot Books, 1995.

Tangvald, Christine. *Fun-to-Do Devotions for Preschoolers Series*. Elgin, IL: David C. Cook, 1991.

Tracking Your Walk. Seattle, WA: YWAM Publishing, 1995.

Williams, Carla. *The Children's Discovery Bible Devotions*. Colorado Springs: Chariot Victor, 1997.

Williams, Carla. *My Bible Dress-up Book*. Colorado Springs: Cook Communications, 2000.

Appendix B

DEVOTIONAL PLAY
ACTIVITIES FOR INFANTS
AND YOUNG CHILDREN

Many parents have told me they do not know how to relate to their infants and young children, yet they naturally want to encourage their child's growth in motor and language skills. There are many wonderful books on the market that provide ideas for interacting with children. This section gives suggestions to help parents see how they can point their children toward the Lord. By beginning spiritual interaction at a very early age, we can lead our children to trust and faith in the Lord. Ecclesiastes 3:11 tells us that God has "set eternity in the hearts of men." The following activities are suggestions that help parents awaken the eternity in their child's heart as they interact and teach him.

Learning Games for Infants

♥ **Hugs and Kisses**: Probably the most important way your child learns during the early months of life is through physical contact. Studies have proven that premature babies develop and gain weight faster when they are touched and cuddled. Through stroking and skin-to-skin contact, you teach your baby to trust his environment, to trust you and eventually to trust in the Lord.

❤ **Eyes and Ears:** "Ears that hear and eyes that see—the LORD has made them both" (Proverbs 20:12). Hold your baby securely in front of you, supporting his head with your hand. Place his face about twelve inches from yours. As soon as your child glances at you, start talking to him. Talk very softly. Say his name. Tell him how much you love him. Quote your favorite Scripture verse to him. Soon you'll notice that your baby is focusing on your face. (Don't worry if he doesn't do this the first time; he may be sleepy or distracted. Try again later.)

Tie bells to your baby's booties or a wrist rattle on his arm. Babies quickly connect their eyes to their hands and feet. He will soon realize that waving his arms or kicking his legs gets results in the tinkling of bells. Begin now to sing songs that focus on God's mercy and love.

❤ **Happy Faces:** "A happy heart makes the face cheerful" (15:13). Here is a game that I used to play with my disabled kids: When your baby is between two and six weeks old, stick your tongue out at him. (Don't worry that you're teaching bad habits—he'll learn plenty on his own!) Stick your tongue in and out a few times. Try other facial expressions. It will surprise you how quickly he will start mimicking your expressions. When my own children came along, it amazed me to find out how early a newborn child responds.

Although your baby cannot understand words at this age, your facial expressions have already become a major way of communication for him. As he grows older, he will learn to judge your moods by your facial expressions. (Ask my teens. They can tell instantly by my face if their behavior is upsetting me.)

❤ **Make a Joyful Noise unto the Lord:** The growth and changes in your baby's language and speech skills can be very exciting. His first expression of communication was undoubtedly a loud cry. Yet as the weeks progress, he learns that he can rock his tongue back and forth to produce cooing sounds. All babies, no matter where they live, start making the same sounds. As the child learns to imitate the sounds his parents make, he will learn his native language. I always thought it would be wonderful if one of my kids would say "Abba" as their first word. But "Da Da" always seems to come first and I decided it's close enough.

When your baby starts cooing, repeat the sound to him. Or get him started by saying a vowel sound to him (ah-ah-ah) in a sing-song tone of voice. Be patient and your baby will begin to "talk" to you.

❤ **Peek-a-Boo:** Play hide-and-seek by covering baby's head with a soft towel or cloth. Say, "Where's Baby?" Baby will squeal with delight as he pulls the towel off his head. Repeat the game, but place the towel over your head and say, "Where's Mommy?" or "Where's Daddy?" This activity teaches your child that he is separate from you. As he grows independent from you, pray that he grows dependent on the Lord. He will learn that you are still there even though he cannot see you and will soon know God is there, too.

Learning Games for Preschoolers

❤ **God Made the Colors:** Draw a large rainbow on poster board using basic colors of red, green, blue, yellow and orange. Encourage your child to sort colored blocks by putting the red ones on the red-colored stripe, blue ones on the blue stripe and so on. Ask questions like, "What color goes here?" to encourage language skills. Talk about how God made light and colors. Read the story of Noah and talk about how the rainbow reminds us that God keeps His promises.

❤ **God Made the Animals:** Sing (using any tune you like) to your child, "God made the animals, God made the animals. God made the animals and me." Then say, "Let's fly like a bird" as you flap your arms and move around the room. Encourage your child to imitate your actions. Repeat the activity with other animals: frog jumping, kittens crawling, rabbit hopping, elephant walking (extend your arm out in front of you as a trunk and walk bent over.)

❤ **I See Something That God Made:** Take your child for a walk outdoors. Ask the child to point to an object that you are describing. Give two clues—one about color or size and one about what it does or how it moves. For instance, "I see something that God made that is white and floats in the sky." The child can call out and point to the clouds. For an indoor version, change it to "I see something that I can thank God for." Use objects like clothing, food, toys or family pictures.

❤ **Feely Meely**: Place several familiar objects like a block, ball or furry toy into a bag. Have your child reach into the bag and describe how the object feels. Talk with your child about how God made our hands so that we could feel so many things. Teach your child words like soft, fuzzy and smooth by playing this game. You can carefully use other objects such as seashells, rocks or leaves and discuss how God made so many wonderful things for us to feel.

Songs

There are lots of great songbooks and tapes on the market that parents can use to learn biblical songs. Many of the songs I used with the Quiet Time Box (Appendix C) were ones I made up to the tunes of familiar songs.

You may not think you are much of a singer, but if I can do it, so can you. After my boys had entered high school, they were talking one day about how I sang and danced with them all the time when they were younger. One of them piped up and said, "What happened to your voice? It sounded a lot better when I was little."

Creation Song

Show your child pictures depicting the days of creation as you sing this song. You can make up any tune you want. I think it changed many times while my children grew up.

Day one, day one, God made light where there was none
Day one, day one, God made light where there was none

Day two, day two, God made skies and seas of blue
Day two, day two, God made skies and seas of blue

Day three, day three, God made plants, flowers and trees
Day three, day three, God made plants, flowers and trees

Day four, day four, God made the sun, moon and stars galore
Day four, day four, God made the sun, moon and stars galore

Day five, day five, God made fish and birds alive
Day five, day five, God made fish and birds alive

Day six, day six, God added man and animals to the mix
Day six, day six, God added man and animals to the mix

Day seven, day seven, God is resting in His heaven
Day seven, day seven, God is resting in His heaven

Animal Song

Sing this song to the tune of "Old McDonald Had a Farm" as you hand toy animals to your child.

Long ago the Lord made the earth, Praise His Name
And on the earth He put some cows, Praise His Name
With a moo moo here and a moo moo there.
There moo, here a moo, everywhere a moo moo.
Long ago the Lord made the earth, Praise His Name

Replace "cow" with other animals names such as cat, dog or horse.

Elementary Age Activities

At this stage children begin to have lives apart from the family. They have activities outside of the home, such as soccer games and music lessons. As you teach your children to practice the spiritual disciplines you have to become more creative in keeping their attention at the elementary age level. Several generations ago many families worked together on farms, with few interruptions of their home life from outside activities. Today parents have to make a conscious decision to spend time with their children. Here are some suggestions for helping elementary-age children to focus on the Lord.

♥ **Puppet Show:** Have older children make finger puppets by cutting off the fingers of rubber or cloth gloves. They can draw faces with a felt tip pen on the puppets. They can also make puppets out of stray socks that always turn up. They can glue yarn or buttons on the socks for eyes and hair. Encourage them to pick their favorite Bible story and put on a performance for younger children in the neighborhood or the family.

♥ **Inner Beauty:** At this age kids begin to become concerned with their appearance. Draw a large heart on a poster board. Have children go through magazines and pick out pictures of things that emphasize the outer part of a person, such as hair brushes, clothing or make-up. Have them paste these pictures around the outer edges of the heart. Then ask them to write words inside the heart that describe the things that God looks for in inner beauty, such as kindness, love and honesty.

♥ **Bible Charades**: Write the names of several biblical characters such as Noah, Jonah and David on small pieces of paper. Fold them so they cannot be read and place them in a small paper bag. Have children take turns drawing names from the paper bag and acting out the character without using any sounds. The rest of the family then tries to guess which Bible hero is being portrayed.

♥ **Bible Match Up:** Write names of Bible characters on separate index cards. On other cards, write a word that could be associated with that character (examples: Noah/Ark, Jonah/Whale, Daniel/Lions). Mix up the cards and spread them face down on a table. Have your children turn over two cards at a time. If the cards match then they keep them face-up. If they do not match then they turn them over and try again until they find all the matches.

♥ **Name That Tune:** Hum just a few bars from a familiar hymn or song. Have your child try to name the song. Once the song is identified, sing it together with your child. Then he can hum a few bars of another song and the parent tries to guess the title. This activity helps to pass the time while doing dishes or other chores.

Appendix C

~ ~ ~ ~ ~ ~ ~ ~ ~ ~ ~

THE QUIET TIME BOX

Once you learn to teach your child discipline in his everyday life, establishing a routine of having a daily quiet time comes naturally. Around the age of six months, or when your child is sitting with a little propping up, introduce "The Quiet Time Box." This box contains toys and books used especially during quiet times. Other toys and materials are kept separate or duplicated for other play times.

Using ideas from our Sunday school nursery, several other mothers and I developed a routine that stimulates an infant's motor, language and reasoning skills as it introduces scriptural concepts. I will share some basic ideas here that you can build on to suit your baby's needs.

My friend, Cheryl, whose children grew up with mine, continues to use this idea with infants she baby-sits from non-Christian homes. Their parents do not mind the obvious referrals to Christ and God, because their children acquire so many wonderful skills. Another friend, Sharon, received permission to use the routine at a secular day care where she worked. The parents were overjoyed at the things their infants were learning.

The following basic ten-to-fifteen-minute routine starts at around six months. Add activities as your child's skills grow.

The Quiet Time Box

♥ The "box" can be anything that you can conveniently tuck away each day. I prefer to use a small suitcase.

♥ Sit your child in front of you in a bumper seat or propped up on the floor so that you can get down on his level. Some mothers find that holding a squirmy child works better. I prefer having direct eye contact with the child.

♥ The routine lasts about ten to fifteen minutes and is done at least three times a week—daily, if possible. As your child grows, you can extend the time and activities according to his skills.

♥ A typical Quiet Time Box routine is presented below using basic items. Suggested things to say or sing to your infant are in italics. (Most of the suggested songs are readily available from a children's songbook.) You will undoubtedly come up with your own. With infants, keep the routine consistent, but you can vary it as the child grows.

1. Hold up one finger and move it back and forth like a clock ticking. (When my kids were little, we used a musical wind-up toy clock. The ticking and song drove my husband crazy). Sing a little tune (if I can do it, you can too!):

> *It's time for quiet time again, tick-tock, tick tock.*
> *It's time for quiet time again, tick-tock, tick tock.*
> *It's time for quiet time right now here we go, tick-tock.*

If you can find a musical toy clock such as I used, rearrange these words to fit the tune of the toy. If not, just make up a tune. Soon your child will begin to respond to the song by raising his finger in a tick-tock motion.

2. Hold up a small Bible or a homemade "Bible" of pictures depicting well-known stories like Adam and Eve, Creation, Noah and the birth of Jesus.

The Bible has two parts: The Old Testament and the New Testament. Hold up two fingers, one on each hand. At first touch your child's fingers to emphasize the two parts. Later your child will hold up his own fingers.

Sing the song *B-I-B-L-E.*
The Old Testament tells us stories about Creation and Noah.
Sing the song *Arky, Arky.*

3. Show your child seven pictures illustrating the different days of the Creation story.
Sing the Creation Song (see Appendix B).

4. *God said let there be light, just by His Word, so now we have different colors.* Use blocks or rings to teach colors. Say the colors as you or child stack the rings.
And God said it was good!

5. Place a variety of small animals in a round oatmeal box. Sing the Animal Song (see Appendix B) as you encourage your child to pull animals out of the box one at a time.

6. Other objects depicting the creation that can be placed in the box are artificial flowers and a variety of plastic fruits. Tell your child that God made many wonderful things for us to enjoy. As your child grows, add objects and activities according to his skill level. For example, add puzzles of animals, food or plants to the creation story.

7. Put together a picture book or purchase a book in which a child is emphasizing different body parts. As you turn the pages say in a sing-song voice,
God made me! God made me!
Two eyes! Blinking eyes! See you with my own two eyes!
(Touch the baby's facial features as you name the parts. Child will soon be naming them himself.)
Left ear! Right ear! I can hear with my two ears! (Ring a rattle or bell by child's ears.)

I have a nose! I can smell a sweet rose! (Use an artificial rose sprayed with perfume for child to smell).

Two hands, two hands! I can clap my own two hands. (Clap child's hands.)

Two arms, two arms! I can hug you with my two arms. (Hug child.)

Two legs, two legs! I like to kick with my two legs! (Touch baby's legs).

8. *Now let's talk about the New Testament. The New Testament tells us about Jesus.* Show the child a picture of Jesus as a baby. To the familiar tune of "Happy Birthday" sing:

> *Baby Jesus was born,*
> *Baby Jesus was born,*
> *Baby Jesus was born in Bethlehem.*

Say: *Just as you were born a baby, Jesus was born as a baby too.*

9. *Jesus grew to be a man and He loves you.* Place a small hand mirror in front of your child and sing "Jesus Loves Me." *Who does Jesus love? He loves [child's name]. Jesus loves everyone!*

10. Show the child a variety of pictures of children from around the world. I had a nesting toy that was the shape of the world with little children that fit inside. Sing "Jesus Loves the Little Children."

11. *The greatest thing Jesus did for us was to die on the cross.* Show the child a picture of Jesus on the cross. *But He did not stay dead in the grave. He rose and went to heaven.* Cut and paste a picture of Jesus ascending in the clouds (easily found in a child's coloring book) onto a plastic straw. As you talk to your child, slowly raise the picture up above your child's head. (He'll follow your movements.) *Come back soon, Lord Jesus. Praise*

the Lord! Raise your hands in praise. Your child will soon imitate your actions.

12. Have your child fold his hands in praying position. *Let's pray. Thank You, Lord, for Your Bible that tells us about Jesus, Your Son.*

Making the Transition from The Quiet Time Box

Remember that the point of the Quiet Time Box is to teach children the basic lessons about the Bible and Jesus Christ. Our goal is to help the child establish the habit of a daily time in God's Word and prayer. While the Quiet Time Box is fun and entertaining, our desire is for the child to set his mind on the things of Christ. If you begin to notice that your child seems to get bored or restless during the routine, add new activities, songs and toys. For example, you can begin to teach your child to name the books of the Bible or at least the four Gospels—Matthew, Mark, Luke and John. Add stories from the Old Testament about Abraham and Sarah, Joseph, or David and Goliath.

If your child begins the Quiet Time routine around six months, by the age of two he may be ready to graduate to a more traditional quiet time. You can, however, begin the Quiet Time Box routine at any time under the age of four.

Make the transition from the Quiet Time routine by putting together a photo album or a three-ring binder of pictures that are similar to the objects in The Quiet Time Box. Put in the album pictures of Creation, the story of Jesus, family and "things we are thankful for." Flip through these pages as you go through the Quiet Time routine.

I made albums entitled "My Day with Jesus" which had pictures of things the child would do each day. The pictures included praying, sharing, eating, playing, reading the Bible and sleeping. We had another album with pictures about God's house, telling the story of what we do at church. These pictures included praying, tithing, sharing, singing and reading the Bible. I used coloring book pictures for all these albums. If you have access to computer graphics, you can find pictures that work great, especially for the Creation story. Be creative and design your own Quiet Time books for your children.

Around the age of four or five you can drop the toys and the albums for a more traditional devotional time. Begin to spend your Quiet Times with your child by reading a Bible story (I always read a verse or two straight from the Bible, along with a Bible storybook) and praying. As your child grows, look for signs that he can be left alone to have Quiet Times apart from you. Help him to choose his own private "prayer closet" where he can pray. Provide age-appropriate devotionals as listed in Appendix A. Enjoy watching your child grow into an intimate relationship with the Lord.

ENDNOTES

Chapter 1

1. Arnold A. Dallimore, *Susanna Wesley: The Mother of John and Charles Wesley* (Grand Rapids, MI: Baker, 1993), p. 57.

2. Ibid.

Chapter 2

1. Richard Foster, *Celebration of Discipline*, revised edition (San Francisco: Harper San Francisco, 1988), p. 20.

2. Thomas à Kempis, *The Imitation of Christ* (Chicago: Moody Press, 1980), p. 63.

3. Foster, p. 144.

Chapter 3

1. Jan Johnson, *Living a Purpose-Full Life* (Colorado Springs: WaterBrook, 1999), p. 16.

2. Tim Williams, *The Essential Piece: Living Luke 14:26 in Everyday Life* (Enumclaw, WA: WinePress, 2000), p. 25.

Chapter 4

1. Grace Ketterman, *Parenting the Difficult Child* (Nashville: Thomas Nelson, 1994), pp. 20-21.

2. William Sears, *Parenting and Child Care* (Nashville: Thomas Nelson, 1993), p. 320.

3. Foster, p. 40.

4. Brother Lawrence, *The Practice of the Presence of God* (New Kensington, PA: Whitaker House, 1982), p. 57.

5. Richard Foster, *Prayers from the Heart* (San Francisco: Harper San Francisco, 1994), p. xv.

Chapter 5

1. Wayne A. Wilson, *Worldly Amusements: Restoring the Lordship of Christ in Our Entertainment Choices* (Enumclaw, WA: WinePress, 1999), pp. 268-269.

2. Jan Johnson, *When the Soul Listens* (Colorado Springs: NavPress, 1999), p. 59.

3. A.W. Tozer, *The Pursuit of God* (Camp Hill, PA: Christian Publications, 1993), pp. 48-49.

4. Aletha Hinthorn, *Filled with His Glory* (Kansas City, MO: Beacon Hill Press, 1999), p. 17.

5. Foster, pp. 96-97.

6. Johnson, *When the Soul Listens*, p. 80.

7. Brother Lawrence, p. 43.

Chapter 6

1. Johnson, *Living a Purpose-Full Life*, p. 19.

2. Foster, p. 128.

Chapter 7

1. Thomas à Kempis, *The Imitation of Christ* (North Brunswick, NJ: Bridge-Logos Publishers, 1999), p. 80.

2. Nancy Parker Brummett, *Simply the Savior* (Colorado Springs: Chariot Victor, 1998), pp. 89-90.

Chapter 9

1. Brother Lawrence, p. 32.

Chapter 10

1. Tim Williams, *The Whisper Revival: Our Only Option* (Enumclaw, WA: Wine-Press Publishing, 2000), p. 34.

2. Roy Hession, *The Calvary Road* (Fort Washington, PA: Christian Literature Crusade, 1950), p. 48.